90 STORY-DEVOTIONS FOR WOMEN

At My Right Hand

DAVALYNN SPENCER

WILSON CREEK PUBLISHING

Unless otherwise indicated, Scripture quotations are taken from the *Holy Bible*, New Living Translation, copyright ©1996, 2004, 2015 by Tyndale House Foundation. Used by permission of Tyndale House Publishers, Carol Stream, Illinois 60188. All rights reserved.

Scripture quotations marked TPT are from The Passion Translation®. Copyright © 2017, 2018, 2020 by Passion & Fire Ministries, Inc. Used by permission. All rights reserved. ThePassionTranslation.com.

Scripture quotations marked NKJV are taken from the New King James Version. Copyright 1982 by Thomas Nelson, Inc. Used by permission. All rights reserved.

Scripture quotations marked NIV are taken from the Holy Bible, New International Version, NIV. Copyright 1973, 1978, 1984, 2011 by Biblica, Inc. Used by permission of Zondervan. All rights reserved worldwide. www.zondervan.com. The "NIV" and "New International Version" are trademarks registered in the United States Patent and Trademark Office by Biblica, Inc.

Scripture quotations marked MSG are taken from *THE MESSAGE*, copyright 1993, 2002, 2018 by Eugene H. Peterson. Used by permission of NavPress. All rights reserved. Represented by Tyndale House Publishers, a Division of Tyndale House Ministries.

Scripture quotations marked TLB are taken from The Living Bible copyright 1971. Used by permission of Tyndale House Publishers, Carol Stream, Illinois 60188. All rights reserved.
All emphasis in Scripture is the author's.

Wilson Creek Publishing

Cover Design and Interior Formatting by 100Covers.

Contents

Preface

I have set the LORD always before me;
Because He is at my right hand I shall not be moved.

Psalm 16:8 NKJV

How can God be ahead of me and right beside me at the same time? Well, He can because He's God.

Since He lives outside of time, unconstrained by clock and calendar, He's already around the bend. He's already where I'm going, and He knows what I'll need when I get there.

Only God can pull that off.

Do we meet God in the past? No, because we can't get there.

Do we meet Him in the future? No, we can't get there either.

Only in the moment, right now, can we connect with Him. Maybe that's why the apostle Paul wrote, "*Now* is the day of salvation" (2 Corinthians 6:2 NKJV).

Because of God's unfettered existence, He can be "always before me," ahead of me leading, yet also "at my right hand," with me every step of the way.

I believe He leaves us messages in His creation that relate directly to His presence in our lives—fingerprints and footprints, if you will.

God reveals His presence to us, but sometimes His footprints are so obscured, we don't recognize them. Or we're too bruised and wounded to find them through the turmoil and tears.

This book of story-devotions is designed to help you recognize God's footprints and experience how close He really is.

At My Right Hand follows my first devotional book, *Always Before Me.* Both titles come from Psalm 16:8 and are drawn from personal daily experiences. May this book inspire you to see that when we walk with Him, the dust on our feet is also on His.

Take a moment each day to meet with Him through these brief story-devotions, Scripture verses, and prayers. When we choose God and His way, we'll find that He is right there with us—at our right hand.

Davalynn Spencer

Day One

Snake in the Grass

For the LORD watches over the path of the godly.

Psalm 1:6

Deciding to take advantage of the morning's warmer weather, I donned my cut-offs, T-shirt, and flip flops and set out to pull weeds along the edge of my driveway. No one walked there because of a wild rose bush and spreading ground cover, but the weeds in between things sprang up as if they'd been invited.

Something else was there that had not been invited, but it took me a minute to notice, for it blended perfectly with its weedy surroundings.

A baby rattlesnake.

Startled, I froze, expecting the tell-tale buzz, but nothing happened. Something was wrong, in particular its lack of movement. Snakes see us before we see them, yet this one was not reacting.

I slowly inched back to the wheel barrow where I'd left a pair of long shears, picked them up, and nudged the snake. It was dead.

Regardless, I ended my weeding project. I'd never heard of an only-child rattlesnake family, and I didn't want to meet the siblings, or Mom either.

That was the last time I did that sort of yard work in shorts and flip flops, regardless of the heat. Boots, jeans, and garden gloves are now required for working along the edges of the yard. I also make sure to keep the wide-open spaces mowed down. And no more cutting across the field when out for a walk. I'll be staying on the path.

Why?

Because we live in snake country and snakes aren't usually on the path.

Since finding the young rattler so close to my house, a favorite verse has taken on even deeper meaning:

You will show me the path of life.
Psalm 16:11 NKJV

Lord, I find comfort in knowing that You will lead me in the path of Your choosing. When I follow You, You go before me, taking care of any threat in the way. When I walk with You, You are right beside me, leading me in the safe way, not through the weeds and brush where danger hides. Thank you, Lord. Amen.

Seek his will in all you do,
and he will show you which path to take.

Proverbs 3:6

Day Two

Great Expectations?

I know the thoughts that I think toward you,
saith the LORD, thoughts of peace,
and not of evil, to give you an expected end.

Jeremiah 29:11 KJV

Expectations were poison in my child-rearing years. I expected my children to do and say certain things the way I wanted them to, and I was upset when they did not.

That might not sound unreasonable for a parent who is raising pre-adults. After all, there are certain scenarios in which children must respond as they are taught, not only for their own good but for that of others as well.

Yet how many times did I hear the Lord whisper in my heart, "Are you letting your expectations get in the way?"

That's when I started learning the difference between expectation and expectancy. They are not the same thing, and I'm still learning the finer details of their differences.

- **Expectation** weights my foot on the gas pedal because I need to arrive at an appointed time.
- **Expectancy** allows me to enjoy the ride, respond to careless drivers without elevating my blood pressure—or hand—and consider the view.
- **Expectation** calls for a predetermined outcome and, if not met, can sow seeds of resentment.
- **Expectancy** eagerly anticipates what lies ahead.

When God reveals Himself to us, anticipation often follows and we might ask, "What will He do?"

- **Expectancy** allows us to stand in awe of His grace and power and love, acknowledging that He is sovereign.
- **Expectation** stamps its foot and demands that God do things our way.

A more recent translation of Jeremiah 29:11 reads, "'For I know the plans I have for you,' says the LORD. 'They are plans for good and not for disaster, to give you a future and a hope.'"

The phrase *a future and a hope* is in most modern translations today and replaces "expected end." But the original Hebrew defines *expected* as something like a cord attached to us, or something that we long for.

What might God have in store for me if I live in expectancy rather than expectation?

What might happen if I trust Him enough to let go of my expectations and leave the

outcome to Him?

Thank you, Lord, for Your encouragement. Thank You for the sense of *expectancy* in Your leading, in the sweet anticipation of Your unlimited reach, infinite knowledge, and unfailing love. Amen.

For we walk by faith, not by sight.
2 Corinthians 5:7 NKJV

Day Three

Circling the Wagons

Be still, and know that I am God.
Psalm 46:10 NKJV

Thirty days after my first husband's debilitating fall, my heart stopped when I saw the hospital number displayed on my buzzing cell phone. I feared the worst, but it was only the nurse helping him to call me.

During those early days, I appreciated caller ID and usually didn't answer other calls. I cherished my friends whose hearts and prayers wove together into a hammock of God's grace that held me close to Him.

But I couldn't always answer the phone.

I was circling the wagons.

Like early settlers did each night of their long journey west, I circled my metaphorical wagons, creating a secure place for myself, protection from outsiders.

In my heart, I hunkered down beneath rough-board bellies and peeked out through the lower spokes of massive wooden wheels.

In the mornings, I'd build a fire in the wood stove and sit in front of it with the house payment, utility statement, and other bills. If the phone rang, caller ID let me know if it was someone who wanted to help. It blessed me, but I hoped they understood if I didn't always answer.

Over time, I learned that it was okay to be unavailable. I learned to silence the phone, put down the bills, and pick up my Bible.

I learned to let the dancing fire comfort me and the quiet fill me.

The peace of His presence would close in around me like circled wagons. And I'd lean toward the warmth of the fire, as if leaning into Him.

For He was there.

Thank You, Lord, for always being there. Thank You for Your faithfulness to send help and comfort and provision. Thank You that when all else falls away, You remain. You are my shelter. Amen.

Those who live in the shelter of the Most High
will find rest in the shadow of the Almighty.
This I declare about the LORD: He alone is my refuge,
my place of safety; he is my God, and I trust him.

Psalm 91:1–2

Day Four

Be a Tree

Then all the trees of the woods
will rejoice before the LORD.

Psalm 96:12 NKJV

If you could be a tree, what kind would you be?

I love pine and cedar, the way the wind sings through their branches and snow settles on them like a puffy quilt. Yet nothing compares to the golden coins of aspens in the fall, glimmering on the high slopes of Colorado's mountains.

Apple, pear, and peach trees grow around my home, and other glorious trees provide shade during summer's hot days.

A giant cottonwood stands guard nearby, and I walk beneath its protective branches each morning – a silent skeleton in winter, barren and cold, and rustling with budding green in spring.

In summer, its full leaves sing, even in a light breeze. Each leaf responds, and the combined whispers raise a chorus akin to a "rushing, mighty wind" (Acts 2:2 NKJV)

As I pass the tree, I think of Psalm 1.

Blessed is the man
Who walks not in the counsel of the ungodly,
Nor stands in the path of sinners,
Nor sits in the seat of the scornful;
But his delight is in the law of the LORD,
And in His law he meditates day and night.
He shall be like a tree planted by the rivers of water,
That brings forth its fruit in its season,
Whose leaf also shall not wither;
And whatever he does shall prosper.

Psalm 1:1–3 NKJV

The tree described by the Psalmist is never a silent winter tree. Not even a spring or fall tree, but a full-leafed tree of summer whose leaves never wither. It offers wind song and shade and comfort. Why?

Because it is planted by the river—one of God's metaphors for life.

I think we have a choice of what kind of tree we want to be. Our roots can reach down deep into the soil of God's marvelous love and we can drink from His water of life whenever we choose. We can be a summer tree, full of life and song.

God's word-pictures surround us, reminding us of His accessibility.

If you could be any kind of tree, which would you choose?

Thank You, Lord, for helping me grow in Your ways, Your truth, and Your promises. Show me how to be the best kind of _____ tree that brings praise to You. Amen.

The righteous will flourish like a palm tree,
they will grow like a cedar of Lebanon;
planted in the house of the Lord, they will flourish in
the courts of our God.

Psalm 92:12–13 NIV

Day Five

Bloom Where You're Planted

For with God, nothing shall be impossible.
Luke 1:37 KJV

Nearly everyone has heard the optimistic adage, "Bloom where you're planted." And even though it's become cliché, most of us try to follow its advice.

But what if our environment is harsh and lifeless? What if we're all alone? What if we're in a place we really don't want to be?

Just beyond my front door sits an old grinding wheel that belonged to my father. I have a pot of petunias on the seat and a pot of geraniums nearby. Due to the southern exposure and stony atmosphere, those potted plants require water twice a day in order to survive summer's heat. Yet, beneath the wheel, rising from the weed-barrier cloth and gravel-covered landscaping is a healthy, blooming, pale pink volunteer petunia. And I've no idea where it came from.

I first saw the valiant seedling during Colorado's monsoon-May rains and nearly pulled it out along with other weeds. (So much for the weed-barrier cloth.) However, the leaves were pale green and soft, so I left it to see what would develop.

I thought it might be a petunia, but I have never planted pale pink petunias. Then I decided it was a morning glory and delighted at the thought of it twining around the antique grinding stone.

Nope. No twining vines or trumpet-like blooms. Regardless of what it was, the seed from which it sprouted chose the most unlikely place to grow—a brutal environment with high radiant-heat temperatures and a lack of water.

Yet it thrived, gently reminding me that with God, all things are possible, even surprises.

I'm convinced that God leaves us messages in His creation that relate directly to His presence in our lives.

What have you seen lately that reminds you of God's surprises and miraculous life-giving nature?

_____

_____

_____

_____

_____

_____

Thank You, Lord, for Your patience with me and for loving me so much that You place reminders in my path. Amen.

For ever since the world was created,
people have seen the earth and sky.
Through everything God made,
they can clearly see his invisible qualities—
his eternal power and divine nature.
So they have no excuse for not knowing God.

Romans 1:20

Day Six

Soak It Up

O God, you are my God; I earnestly search for you.
My soul thirsts for you; my whole body longs for you
in this parched and weary land where there is no water.

Psalm 63:1

Sometimes I just want to be a sponge.

Not the kind that scrubs grout in the shower or scum around the sink. I want to be a human sponge that gets to lie back and soak up the sunshine. Soak up the ambiance of a nice restaurant, the romance of a good movie, the beauty of a crimson sunset over the Rocky Mountains.

Sometimes I don't want to participate, make an extra effort, contribute to whatever-it-is—I just want to soak it in.

I confess, that's a pretty lazy attitude. And when I'm tired or stressed, it gets worse, as it did several years ago after a debilitating injury to a loved one. My desperate need for a break from it all sent me to a three-day writer's conference in Texas.

While driving to the airport, I told the Lord I wanted to be a sponge when I got there. Just soak everything in rather than worry about pitching my book ideas to publishers. I didn't want to interview or be interviewed. I was tired of performing.

Leaning back in my narrow window seat for the two-hour flight, I considered how self-centered the sponge idea was. Sheesh—me, me, me. Get all I can. Had I really fallen that far?

And then God corrected me, but not in the way I expected.

"What does a sponge do when it's squeezed?" He asked my weary spirit.

Well, it *gives*, I suppose.

It drips out on whatever's nearby.

It can give a drink to the thirsty, like soldiers offered Jesus on the cross.

It can cool a body, as I did with my feverish toddler years before.

Wipe away the dirt. Cleanse.

"Yes," He whispered. "Be a sponge. But soak up *Me*. And when you're squeezed, I'll come out to those around you."

God's compassion overwhelmed me. We *are* sponges; I just hadn't seen it from His perspective. He created us to be porous. We absorb and we leak.

Everything we listen to, read, and watch seeps into us and forms patterns in our thoughts and dreams. Is it good? Is it of Him?

How right He was when He said, "Soak up Me." How desperately I need Him.

Thank You, Lord, for Your incomparable mercy and grace. Wash over me and fill me with You. Amen.

I thirst for God, the living God.
When can I go and stand before him?

Psalm 42:2

Day Seven

Cold Shoulder

Trust in the LORD with all your heart
and lean not on your own understanding;
in all your ways submit to him,
and he will make your paths straight.

Proverbs 3:5–6 NIV

Annie and Oakley were my two teenaged tabby mousers. Litter mates and identical in appearance, I could tell them apart only by their attitudes. On that point, they were as different as salt and pepper. Especially when it came to the matter of trust.

Annie trusted me, Oakley did not. To say Oakley was skittish would be an understatement. I couldn't get within ten feet of her.

When these pubescent female felines arrived in their portable kennel, I was an unknown. Their eyes were dark and wide with fear, and they hid behind anything they could find.

In my attempt to make them feel welcomed, I left them food and left them alone. They left me a mouse one morning, right next to their dish. A fair trade.

Annie soon warmed to me, running her little "motorboat" as my mother used to call a cat's purr. Because of her trust, Annie slept in the garage at night, high atop stacked tubs in a soft kitty bed.

Oakley slept outside beneath the low-spreading juniper and dashed in each morning when I opened the garage door. Wet if it rained, cold from the night, and always hungry, she would scurry in and up to the dryer where the cat food dish sat beyond the reach of our dog, Blue.

I never shut Oakley out. Each night I called her, just like I called Annie, but Oakley didn't come because she didn't trust me. If she had, she would have slept like Annie, dry and cushioned with a midnight snack always at the ready.

Oakley finally started coming in as the autumn weather deteriorated.

Isn't that just like us? Running for shelter when we're forced, rather than stepping into love via trust.

Not unlike God and me. When I trust Him, circumstances always turn out better, and my needs are always met. But more than that, I have the peace of His presence. He loves me, and I'm learning to trust that.

Thank You, God, for Your patience with me. Thank You for Your unfailing love and for being so worthy of my trust. Amen.

He who dwells in the secret place of the Most High
shall abide under the shadow of the Almighty.
I will say of the LORD,
"He is my refuge and my fortress; My God,
in Him I will trust."

Psalm 91:1-2 NKJV

Day Eight

Small Fix, Big Difference

*Catch us the foxes, the little foxes
that ruin the vineyards,
our vineyards that are in bloom.*

Song of Solomon 2:15 NIV

My front door wasn't doing its job other than swinging open and closed. Sort of.

At first, I couldn't get it open without a crowbar (slight exaggeration). A few weeks later, it wouldn't lock (no exaggeration). I jammed a chair under the doorknob at night as an extra precaution.

When I told my father-of-four son about it, he said, "Let me take a look at it."

He looked, said it needed a shim, and asked if I had a piece of cardboard.

Sure I did. As a former elementary school teacher, I had a piece of everything tucked away somewhere.

He removed the door hinges, sized down the cardboard, and slid it behind one of the hinges.

After replacing the screws, he closed the door. Perfectly. The dead bolt slid home with a clunk, and the latch worked.

Not at all the fix I was fearing.

I originally thought I needed a different solution, something major like a new door, or a new lock, which meant new keys. Something that was going to cost me money and time and frustration.

All I needed was a shim — a very small adjustment that made a very big difference.

Thin and often tapered, a shim fills a small space or gap between two things, adding support or providing a better fit. The cardboard my son put behind a hinge raised the entire door so locks and bolts lined up perfectly.

The metaphor hit me like a swinging door.

Successful fixes in our lives are often simple adjustments. Biblically speaking, those simple adjustments reap great dividends. They can also prevent great destruction.

A small change in our words can save a marriage. A small show of appreciation can enrich a relationship.

It's the little things that get under our skin, like a burr beneath a saddle that makes a horse buck and throw its rider. Making the effort to remove those burrs is worth it.

Snide remarks depreciate a person's worth, but a word well-spoken can mend a heart.

"Thank you," "I'm sorry," and "You're right," might be the most neglected shims of human interaction.

Is there something in your life that needs a slight adjustment that could result in a great improvement?

Lord, please show me the small things I can change in the way I talk or respond to others. Give me grace and humility to make the adjustments I need to make. Amen.

A word fitly spoken is like apples of gold in settings of silver.

Proverbs 25:11 NKJV

Day Nine

Power and Authority

*I have given you authority
over all the power of the enemy.*

Luke 10:19

During football season, my husband and I enjoy watching the games.

(Okay, ladies, don't turn the page—stay with me for a minute.)

Professional football games are the easiest place to observe the difference between power and authority.

In a recent game we watched, one team missed catching the ball in the end zone and a player on the opposing team ranted in the face of the referee who—according to that player—missed calling some sort of infraction.

The disgruntled giant of a man bounced up and down and back and forth, dwarfing the calm stripe-shirted official who merely turned and walked away.

The big guy had all the power in the world to squash the much smaller official, but the official had all the authority.

I love that.

It reminds me of what Jesus told His disciples when He sent them out on a faith test-drive and they came back stoked: "I have given you authority over all the power of the enemy" (Luke 10:19). Jesus can bestow this authority to His followers because He has *all* authority given by His Father:

"I have been given all authority in heaven and on earth" (Matthew 28:18).

When the enemy comes after us with his lies, ranting and raving and trying to shake our faith, we can turn our backs on him because Jesus has given us authority over his power.

But that's not all.

Jesus has also given us power too:

"One day Jesus called together his twelve disciples and gave them power and authority to cast out all demons and to heal all diseases" (Luke 9:1).

The key to this is to maintain our connection with God's ultimate power and authority, which we do by regularly reading His Word, praying, and worshipping Him. We can do nothing on our own.

When the enemy rants and raves at us, we can stand on the promises of God. And when we need help, we can tell Jesus. He is the ultimate official.

Thank You, God, for giving me examples of Your power and authority. Thank You that You are stronger and greater than anything the enemy can throw at me. Amen.

By his divine power, God has given us
everything we need for living a godly life.
We have received all of this by coming to know him,
the one who called us to himself
by means of his marvelous glory and excellence.

2 Peter 1:3

Day Ten

Name Dropper

*God elevated him to the place of highest honor
and gave him the name above all other names.*

Philippians 2:9

My friend Jill is a name dropper. She raises registered Nigerian Dwarf goats on her Kentucky farm, Sinai Thunder, and she drops a blessing on each animal born on the farm.

As animal breeders do, Jill gives each kid a name that refers back to the dam and sire, but she makes sure that each name is also a blessing that points to God.

A few examples are Sinai Thunder Chariots of Fire, called Cherry; Sinai Thunder Breath of Heaven, called Heaven; Sinai Thunder Miracle of Grace, called Gracie; and Sinai Thunder AD Luke, called Lukie.

She also has Redemption, Charity, Queen of Sheba, a buck named Agnus Dei, and a truckload of others. Did I mention she has one hundred goats?

When Jill buys a goat from another breeder, the original registered name comes with it, sometimes an uncomfortably negative moniker. However, in her day-to-day handling of the animals, she always drops an unlovely name and blesses each animal with a new name.

One doe's original name was Voodoo Princess. This pretty mama is now called Queenie—an upgrade in status as well as a blessing.

Another doe's registered name is Allamanda, but Jill refers to her as Hallelujah. Every time she jumps on the stanchion to be milked, she does a little Hallelujah dance, prancing in place until given her food. And her daughter, who looks just like her, is named Adoration and called Addie.

After considering the way Jill blesses her kids with godly names, I realized that God did this with His kids too. He dropped names all the time.

Remember Jacob who was renamed Israel? How about Abram and Sarai who became Abraham and Sarah?

In the New Testament, Saul became Paul and Simon became Peter.

Name dropping changed these people's lives.

So I wonder—what names should I be dropping? Have I tagged people with curses rather than blessings?

What do I call the children I'm around? Little Monster? Trouble-maker?

Do I really want a child to carry that label—or worse yet, live up to it?

I plan to do some name dropping in the near future. Let's drop a few blessings on those we come in contact with and see how they change.

Thank You, Lord, for Your beautiful example of blessing people through a name. Please show me how to do this in my own life. Amen.

A good name is to be chosen rather than great riches, loving favor rather than silver and gold.

Proverbs 22:1 NKJV

Day Eleven

Foundation

Everyone who hears these words of mine
and puts them into practice
is like a wise man who built his house on the rock.
The rain came down, the streams rose, and the winds
blew and beat against that house; yet it did not fall,
because it had its foundation on the rock.

Matthew 7:24-25 NIV

Fall winds brush against Colorado's Front Range, swirling aspen leaves with a whispery breath. They also pummel people's homes with gusts that send lawn chairs, trash cans, and fences flying.

Summer rains sprinkle the earth, watering wild grass and flowers, unless they're falling in torrential curtains that wash out roads and tumble car-sized boulders through mountain mudslides.

Both wind and water have two-sided na-tures—soothing and nurturing or destructive and terrifying.

In my creative writing classes, I asked students to show both sides of these natural life forces: Wind as a whispering breeze or a roaring tornado. Water trickling down a stream bed or crashing through a canyon at flood levels.

Handling the harsher extremes in real life isn't quite as easy as describing them on paper. Life situations can pound us into the ground or wash it out from under us—not just physically, but spiritually and emotionally as well.

Jesus knew this and He told us how to withstand the onslaughts. He said that if we put His words into practice, we'd survive the storms the same way a sturdy house built on a rock survives the wind and rain.

It's all about foundation and obedience.

During a hike one day in the hills above my home, I came upon a gnarled cedar tree twisting up from the rocky top of an exposed hill. Extreme winds and rain had distorted the tree into its unique shape. But the tree hadn't washed away or blown off the hilltop. It hadn't let go because its roots were embedded in the rock.

The tree reminded me that if I'm rooted in Jesus, the Rock of my Salvation, together we can weather anything.

Thank You, Lord, for Your rock-solid presence in my life. Help me put Your words into practice and do what You say. Ground me in Your love and faithfulness. Amen.

> *Truly he is my rock and my salvation;*
> *he is my fortress, I will not be shaken.*
> *My salvation and my honor depend on God];*
> *he is my mighty rock, my refuge.*

Psalm 62:6–7 NIV

Day Twelve

Life Wins

The thief comes only to steal and kill and destroy;
I have come so that they may have life.
Whoever drinks the water I give them will never thirst.

John 10:10 NIV, John 4:14 NIV

The prophet Jeremiah said a person who trusts in God will flourish like a tree whose leaves never wither. But he didn't mention anything about being eaten alive.

One spring, I planted an aspen tree cluster in the back yard, watered it faithfully, and strategically placed rock and wire to discourage cats and deer.

However, nothing stopped the grasshoppers.

The critters were worse than I'd ever seen, and with plague-like precision, they took my tree down to nothing but a skinny trunk and stems. I returned to the nursery for a bottle of heavy-duty bug spray I'd never used. But the hoppers were so bad in our area that the spray was on backorder for months out.

"Keep watering your tree," the clerk said. "It's only being defoliated."

I could relate.

Watering a vertical stick in the ground wasn't exactly encouraging, but after faithfully attending to my duty, new growth began to show. The following spring, the little aspen pushed out twice as many leaves as before, and they fluttered in the breeze as only aspen leaves can. But that wasn't all. It had spread underground and sent additional saplings across the back yard. The cluster had grown unseen, and rather than die, it had produced a dozen more little trees.

Aspens don't grow alone, but thrive via an underground, interconnected root system called a clonal colony. One of the largest on earth is said to be an aspen grove in Utah.

Talk about networking!

I was amazed by the regenerative properties that flowed through my aspen tree even though I'd earlier thought it was done in.

Such is the power of life. And such is the power of Christ's life in us.

Sometimes I feel defoliated—as if every fresh and living part of me is being devoured by the enemy. I can almost hear him chewing. The woman's encouragement to "keep watering" was exactly what I needed for the tree and exactly what I need to survive emotionally and spiritually.

Jesus is the water of life, and as I fill up with Him, He faithfully keeps me alive through all seasons of destruction, dormancy, rebirth, and fruition.

Like aspens, Christians are individual from one another, but we are referred to as the body of Christ because we are interconnected by God's Holy Spirit. We support each other, draw upon each other for strength and encouragement, and thrive in each other's company.

And after a particularly heavy onslaught by the enemy, when we think we're done in, if He lives within us, we live too.

Thank You, Lord, for Your miraculous, regenerative life force within us, connecting us to Yourself and to each other. Thank You that life wins! Amen.

May your roots go down deep into
the soil of God's marvelous love.

Ephesians 3:17 TLB

Day Thirteen

Perspective

"For My thoughts are not your thoughts,
Nor are your ways My ways," says the LORD.
'For as the heavens are higher than the earth,
So are My ways higher than your ways,
And My thoughts than your thoughts.

Isaiah 55:8–9 NKJV

Sometimes I miss what's right under my nose. Or above my nose, as the case may be. I take for granted what I am accustomed to seeing and, therefore, I no longer see it.

Can you relate?

I live not far from Pikes Peak. It is commonly referred to as America's Mountain because it served as the inspiration for Katherine Lee Bates's poem-turned-song, "America the Beautiful." After years of driving around its base from east to south, I took a long look at that mountain from a different perspective.

Riding the 8.9-mile Cog Railway out of Manitou Springs to the end of the track on top was the perfect way to see the majestic mountain. No driving winding roads or negotiating hairpin curves. Just a nice scenic route straight up, relatively speaking.

Many lesser ridges reach toward the 14,115-foot pink-granite peak, and the view along the way was unparalleled. Log cabins from the 1800s crumbled into the forest. Fallen trees made room for new growth, and bare rock faces challenged hikers on foot trails. Such things could not be seen from a distance, yet I also saw distance itself at the top. At least it seemed that way while looking east into the state of Kansas.

For too long I had ignored my curiosity and pushed the Cog Railway experience into the corner cabinet I called "Someday." We all know what happens Someday—usually nothing. So I decided, *Why not today?*

It wasn't exactly an unplanned excursion. I had to make reservations and plan accordingly. But I'm glad I made the effort. It was well worth the time to gain a different perspective and new appreciation for the splendor of God's handiwork.

Is there something in your life that you need to see from a different angle? Would you benefit from another perspective of an occurrence or a hurtful retort from a close friend or family member? Seeing things from a different angle can help us discover hidden truths and find solutions to problems we didn't recognize before.

Whatever it is, ask the Lord to help you see what you haven't seen. It may change everything.

Thank You, God, that Your perspective is so different from mine. Help me take the time to see things, and people, the way You see them. Amen.

*Before the mountains were born or you
brought forth the whole world,
from everlasting to everlasting you are God.*

Psalm 90:2 NIV

Day Fourteen

Unless It's Broken

And I will give you a new heart,
and I will put a new spirit in you.
I will take out your stony, stubborn heart
and give you a tender, responsive heart.

Ezekiel 36:26

On freelance assignment for the local newspaper, I attended a craft fair one weekend where talented people displayed their hand-made wares. From quilts and candles to woodcarvings, scarves and paintings, the most intriguing vendors were those who brought their rocks.

They were lapidarists—stone-shaping experts who knew how to distinguish a gem from a plain rock and fashion it into art.

One such man stood behind a glass showcase that held beautifully polished stones in a variety of colors and shapes. Some of the stones were made into brooches and pins, others placed into settings for rings and earrings. However, the most intriguing to me were not his finished products but the rough rocks alongside them—so rough that if I had hiked by them on a mountain path, I might have kicked them out of the way. I certainly would not have recognized them for their hidden potential.

When I asked how he recognized a true gem among thousands of ordinary rocks, he gladly shared his secret:

"You can't tell what it is unless it's broken."

Ouch. The rockslide of spiritual application nearly crushed me.

He continued, "It either has to be broken, or the day has to be rainy." When the sun hit a wet or broken rock just right, that was when he could see what it really was.

A casual observer might see a stone on the path, but a master craftsman sees what it could be.

"Working with it, you develop a feel for it," the vendor said. "You can tell if it's hard or soft, easy to cut or not."

A lapidarist will cut, polish, and possibly engrave the once unappealing stone, transforming it into a beautiful work of art.

Isn't this how God works with us? He knows what we can be, He claims us in our raw and unattractive brokenness, and then He fashions us into living stones. But only if we let Him. He never forces or demands but handles us with the most tender patience.

When we're left broken in the pouring rain of adversity or cracked open beneath merciless oppression, we feel anything but beautiful. Yet the Master Artisan sees us for what we can be at the healing touch of His hand. He can take our ugliness and make us beautiful for His glory.

Thank You, Lord, for seeing beyond our hard and crusty facades to what lies underneath. Thank You for the touch of Your hand that fashions us into lasting beauty that glorifies You. Amen.

And you are living stones that God is building into his spiritual temple.

1 Peter 2:5

Day Fifteen

Are You In or Out?

Give thanks to the God of heaven.
His faithful love endures forever.

Psalm 136:26

Last Monday, the post office was closed for the observance of a holiday. Tuesday morning, the line of postal patrons stretched out the door and into the lobby.

As I approached the end of the queue, I noticed a college-aged man standing off to the side with paperwork in his hand, looking like he'd never been inside a post office before.

"Are you in line?" I asked.

"Sort of," he replied.

Not the answer I expected. I'd thought he would say yes or no.

I set my heavy box on the dividing counter that keeps customers from the main counter until it's their turn, then looked at the young man and indicated the space in front of me. The space he should have occupied.

"Go ahead."

He did.

I don't know the reason for his hesitancy that day. Many things could have kept him in the corner watching the line grow longer. But he reminded me of how dangerous it can be to go through life with a "sort of" attitude.

Some folks drive with that mentality—sort of in their lane. Often couples don't get married because things might not work out. And other people are in a perpetual state of wishy-washy about everything. It's not safe.

Yes, we all look for guidance in our decisions, but once we find it, shouldn't we commit, whether to our convictions or our relationships with other people and with God?

- The Bible mentions this concept several times:
- Choose today whom you will serve (see Joshua 24:15).
- How much longer will you waver between two opinions? (see 1 Kings 18:21).

- You are neither hot nor cold. I wish that you were one or the other! (see Revelation 3:15).

The young man in the post office was getting nowhere until he committed to either get in line or leave.

God has committed Himself to us in His unfailing love.

Jesus didn't "sort of" save us from the penalty of sin.

And we don't have to fear that there is a "sort of" way to heaven.

Let's be more determined in our commitments to God and others—either in or out.

Thank You, God, that You are clear and certain in Your Word, and not wishy-washy. Thank You for committing to us and that Your unfailing love endures forever. Amen.

For the word of the LORD holds true,
and we can trust everything he does.
He loves whatever is just and good;
the unfailing love of the Lord fills the earth.

Psalm 33:4–5

Day Sixteen

Be What?

Be still and know that I am God.

Psalm 46:10 NKJV

There's a lot of clamoring right now. A lot of noise. A lot of posturing and pointing, criticism and chaos. And none of it is new. It has all happened before, many times, in fact. And God's antidote has always been the same:

Be still . . .

Some versions of the Bible read, "stop fighting" or "cease striving."

It's easier said than done.

Our busy lives don't give us much quiet time to reflect, listen, or simply breathe. Things always press in, demanding our attention, whether they are as fleeting as the news and social media, or as important as a spouse or child.

But being still—quiet and undistracted—is critical to our spiritual survival in this world so full of noise. Therefore, we have to *make* time.

This is not an easy assignment, but it's doable. Consider these three suggestions:

- Take a quiet moment in the early morning. Jesus often got up before everyone else and went off by Himself to pray. He was always surrounded by people, yet He made the effort to be alone with His Father. Perhaps He sought direction and balance.
- Go for a walk outside. One of my favorite verses says Jesus went out of the house and sat by the sea. I don't have a sea near my home, but I have a place where I can walk, be quiet, and listen.
- Steal away while the kids are napping—like Susanna Wesley did. The seventeenth-century mother of nineteen (not all survived infancy) found it difficult to get a moment to herself, so she made an "apron escape." When she sat down and pulled her large apron up over her head, her children knew Mother was praying and they must leave her alone. An unusual tactic, but it worked.

These three suggestions go hand in hand with three mandatory requirements:

- Turn off the television/radio.
- Silence the phone.
- Shut down the internet.

It helps when we let the silence in. When the Old Testament prophet Elijah sought God, he found the Creator not in wind, quake, or fire, but in a whisper.

Maybe God won't say anything earth-trembling to you. Maybe He won't say anything more than "I am here." But isn't that what we need the most? To know that He is God, and He is with us.

Thank You, God, that You are bigger than all the noise around us, and that You are always with us. Amen.

And they will call him Immanuel,
which means "God is with us."

Matthew 1:23

Day Seventeen

A Light on My Path

Your word is a lamp for my feet, a light on my path
Psalm 119:105 NIV

Last winter my son sent me a video of his drive to work near Cripple Creek, Colorado, along what is known as Shelf Road. There is a very good reason it's called Shelf Road, or The Shelf, by those hearty souls who travel it every day or night, depending on their shift.

The Shelf was once a toll road from Cañon City, Colorado, to the Cripple Creek gold mining district during the 1890s and early 1900s. Stagecoaches and freight wagons, even ranchers and lone riders, traveled its 13.5-mile stretch. At either end, the road is merely that—a road with gorgeous mountain vistas—until you get to what locals call the "High Shelf."

Sans guardrails, street lights, pavement, pullouts, or a second lane, the High Shelf snakes along sheer cliffs like, well, a shelf.

Once a driver makes it to the High Shelf, commitment comes quite naturally. There is no turning around. No pulling over to the side of the road because there is no side of the road. Only steep rock face on one side, and a severe drop-off on the other.

When driven at night, the adventure reminds me of navigating life by faith.

My son filmed his video at night after a snow storm. The white roadway appeared in roughly two-hundred-foot segments – the distance his headlights reached. At curves, it dropped off into inky blackness until the headlights inched forward, revealing solid ground.

Two hundred feet doesn't sound like much of a buffer zone for moving forward, but it was enough to light the way. As my son progressed, so did the lights, revealing what was ahead, but not what was around the next bend or a hairpin turn.

My son had to have faith that when he reached the next curve, his headlights would show him the way.

Isn't that similar to our faith-walk with the Lord? We want to know our life's route. We want to see around those shadowy turns up ahead, but the Lord says, "Trust Me. I'll get you there."

The psalmist wrote, "Your word is a lamp for my feet, a light on my path." If we stop and think about it, that's a pretty short beam, but it shines onto the most critical part of our journey: where we are at the moment.

God's Word assures us of His presence, and His presence gives us peace and direction.

The next time we find ourselves navigating one of life's High Shelf roads, let's remember that Jesus is our Light. He'll get us where we need to be if we trust Him.

Thank You, Jesus, for being the Light that leads me through life. I know I can trust You. Amen.

He guards the paths of the just and
protects those who are faithful to him.

Proverbs 2:8

Day Eighteen

NEVER Give Up!

And let us not be weary in well doing:
for in due season we shall reap, if we faint not.

Galatians 6:9 KJV

It had been several months—a season, in fact—since I'd bought coffee at our church's in-house coffee shop. That morning, I needed a cup of pumpkin-spice latte.

I'd not received an anti-splash sticker in the past. Maybe it was a new thing they'd started. But that morning, a sticker atop my plastic lid said
NEVER *give up!*
Not *Never give up*, but **NEVER** *give up!*
A clear command.
As an educator, I avoided the words *never* and *always* in the classroom, for students invariably come up with exceptions. It never failed. I mean . . . it seldom, if ever, failed.
Yet, there it was, *that word,* glaring up at me from the black plastic lid of my paper coffee cup.

My first sticker from what we called the Connections Café, arriving at an iffy point in my life.

Coincidence?

Never.

I believe God was paying attention and orchestrated the whole thing for my benefit. He can do that, you know. Put a coin in a fish's mouth. Make a donkey colt available for a ride into town.

The server that morning could have given me a different sticker, one with a bird or a smiley face or a rainbow, rather than the one I needed.

I took it personally.

I needed encouragement during those difficult days, yet I tended to avoid people. Grieve privately. Sit by myself.

God, in His omnipotence, broke through my self-imposed barrier.

Finding a solitary seat in the sanctuary, I carefully removed the sticker and applied it to the inside back cover of my Bible. And to my weary heart.

Thank You, God, for Your great and perfect love. Thank you for seeing me and loving me with all my baggage. Thank You for putting people in my path with encouraging words. Amen.

Kind words are like honey—
sweet to the soul and healthy for the body.

Proverbs 16:24

Day Nineteen

You Are What You Eat

But Jesus replied, "I have a kind of food
you know nothing about."

John 4:32

When I was growing up, my mother told me, "You are what you eat." The phrase seemed silly at the time, but I couldn't argue with the results of eating too much ice cream compared to eating a decent meal. As I matured into adulthood, the difference was accentuated. When I ate healthy foods, I became healthier and stronger. When I ate junk food, I was lethargic and listless.

Over the years I found the same "transfer" to occur in the entertainment foods I ingest, whether books, movies, or television programs. I tend to think, speak, and act like that which I steadily consume.

In early computer-speak, I believe the phrase was "garbage in, garbage out."

If this concept is consistently true, and I believe it is, then what I "feed" my mind and spirit is as important a choice as what I feed my body.

A short New Testament book called Philippians gives me a pretty good grocery list. I especially like *The Message* version:

Summing it all up, friends, I'd say you'll do best
by filling your minds and meditating on things true,
noble, reputable, authentic, compelling, gracious —
the best, not the worst;
the beautiful, not the ugly; things to praise,
not things to curse. . . . Do that, and God,
who makes everything work together,
will work you into his most excellent harmonies.

Philippians 4:8–9 MSG

We have quite a social smorgasbord from which to choose nowadays. There is a lot being said. There is a lot to hear. Theories abound, many of them empty and useless, fragile shells with nothing on the inside.

Direction and peace, health and balance are priceless commodities found nowhere but in God.

So I pass on to you what has been passed down to me: you are what you eat. Familiarize yourself with what God has to say. Choose His ways, feast at His table, and become strong in Him.

Thank You, Lord, for knowing what I need to survive both physically and spiritually. Thank You for providing Your Word for my spirit. You make me whole. Amen.

My son, give attention to my words;
incline your ear to my sayings.
Do not let them depart from your eyes;
keep them in the midst of your heart;
For they are life to those who find them,
and health to all their flesh.

Proverbs 4: 20–22 NKJV

Day Twenty

Hide-and-Seek

Even the darkness is not dark to you;
the night is bright as the day,
Darkness and light are the same to you.

Psalm 139:12

When my youngest granddaughter was three years old, she loved playing hide-and-seek. Without fail, her giggling or wiggling toes gave her away. Mom, Dad, and I could always find her.

When she couldn't see us, she was certain that we couldn't see her. She wasn't hiding in fear, she was hiding in fun. But don't we hide from our heavenly Father in a similar way, thinking He can't see us?

As His grownup children, we often try to hide from God when guilt shines its floodlight on us. We start to believe that He can't see us when embarrassment, fear, or pride send us running away. We may stop looking for Him, meeting Him for quiet times alone, or reading the promises and guidance He has given us in Scripture.

We try to cover up our hearts, hoping He can't see inside, forgetting that He knows everything about us including where we are.

The same thing happened to Adam and Eve in the garden of Eden when they picked and ate fruit from the only tree that God said they must not touch. They could eat from all the others, but not that one.

Guilty consciences sent them running for cover. When the Lord strolled through the garden that evening, He called to Adam, "Where are you?"

Did God ask that question because He didn't know where Adam was? Or could He have asked it for Adam's benefit? Maybe it was His way of assuring Adam and Eve that no matter what they had done, even in disobedience, He still sought them out. He still wanted to be with them.

God waits for us to run *to* Him, not *from* Him.

The great singer of Israel wrote: "You know when I sit down or stand up. You know my thoughts even when I'm far away" (Psalm 139:2).

If He knows our thoughts, I'm pretty sure He knows everything else too, yet He loves us just the same.

Have you found yourself hiding from God lately? Try running *to* Him. He's waiting for you with open arms.

Thank You, God, for loving me even when I fail. Thank You for making a way back to You through the sacrifice and blood of Jesus shed on the cross for me. Thank You that I can hide in You. Amen.

You are my hiding place.

Psalm 32:7 NIV

Day Twenty-One

All for Good

Oh, taste and see that the LORD is good;
blessed is the man who trusts in Him!

Psalm 34:8 NKJV

As a novelist, I write books with characters who face trials and struggles similar to what real people face every day. While writing a scene for one of my Western romances, I came face-to-face with my heroine's memories of her mother's favorite saying that "all things work together for good."

The heroine was having trouble believing what her mother had taught.

Bad things had happened to her—a lot of bad things. And they weren't suddenly made good just because she trusted God. The platitude chaffed her sense of fairness.

Her less-than-perfect situation had landed her in a stranger's home where she was doing the best she could. At that particular moment of frustration and disappointment, she was making a cake.

As if standing next to the heroine, I could taste flour dust in the air while she sifted what she needed into a bowl. A person could choke on flour—a tasteless death for certain.

Then she added Baker's chocolate, a bitter ingredient.

Next came sugar, everyone's favorite, but it could make a person sick if eaten in great quantities.

Eggs followed. Not exactly tasty in their raw condition.

None of the ingredients my heroine added to her mixing bowl were appetizing on their own, but when *worked together*, they combined to create a chocolate cake—something very good indeed.

As she poured the batter into a baking pan, she wondered if her efforts reflected what God does in our lives. He takes the bad—the less-than-perfect things—and works them together into something good.

Because *He* is good.

If He can make light and earth and sky from nothing and make man from dirt, imagine what He can do with our wrecked lives and surrendered hearts.

Thank You, Father, that You are good and know how to work things together in our lives in a way that benefits us and glorifies You. Amen.

And we know that all things work together
for good to them that love God,
to them who are the called according to His purpose.

Romans 8:28 NKJV

Day Twenty-Two

What If?

I will be with you.
I will not leave you nor forsake you.

Joshua 1:5 NKJV

This two-word query is one of the most important questions a novelist asks while working on a book project. Various answers can propel an author's character into riveting plot twists or brain-throbbing conflicts.

But when seeking to live a faith-led life of obedience in the real world, "What if?" can be the most destructive, derailing question of all.

Unfortunately, we ask "What if?" all the time when it comes to doing what God tells us to do, because—let's be honest—He's asked His people to do some pretty strange things.

Like, march around a walled city for seven days blowing trumpets.

Or feed a crowd of thousands with a kid's sack lunch.

Or invite our neighbor to church.

Or trust Him.

Sometimes God asks us to be unlike everyone else because He wants to lead us on a different trail, often referred to as a path of righteousness (see Psalm 23:3).

But instead of stepping out in obedience, we start asking, "What if?"

What if it doesn't work?

What if my timing is off?

What if people won't like me?

These worry-inducing, fret-focused questions often stop us in our tracks.

"What if?" racked me up last week, and it had nothing to do with the novel I was writing and everything to do with the trail I was walking.

The turning point arrived when I remembered that I am not alone. The same God who said, "Let there be light," is lighting my path. The same God who told Joshua He wouldn't leave him won't leave me either.

I have found that peace rushes in when I do what God whispers to my heart.

It is a simple, two-step process, just like the old song my parents used to sing: "Trust and Obey."

Left foot, right foot—one step at a time.

It may not be easy, but it really can be that simple.

Because He really is that faithful.

Thank You, God, for Your incomparable faithfulness. Thank You for sticking with me even when I falter and for always seeing me through. Amen.

Let your conduct be without covetousness; be content with such things as you have. For He Himself has said, "I will never leave you nor forsake you."

Hebrew 13:5 NKJV

Day Twenty-Three

My Hiding Place

You are my hiding place;
you will protect me from trouble
and surround me with songs of deliverance.

Psalm 32:7 NIV

Do you ever want to run away? The other day, I did just that.

I ate breakfast at the dining room table rather than my desk. Strange, what we run from.

The break in routine served as my initial escape, and I ate looking out the picture window at the back yard instead of my computer screen.

The wheels in my head slowed. The generator in my gut slackened. My internal pace skipped a step, then wound down to a casual pace. It was good. I needed the reminder that I didn't have to work, work, work.

In one of my books, *The Miracle Tree*, an old, burned-out oak tree stands at the corner of the heroine's property. It lives because its exterior didn't burn. Though it is hollow, it stands tall and graceful with soft green leaves and acorns.

The cavity is large enough for two children to fit inside, backs against the rough bark interior, imagining the greatest adventures.

The tree is real, and it anchors the bottom pasture of the property where I lived for several years in the California foothills.

Later, I found another hollow, living tree along the Riverwalk in Cañon City, Colorado. Each morning that I walked along the singing Arkansas River, the hollow tree called me to crawl inside, lean my back against its rough interior, and hide.

Hide from all the visual noise in my life. The demands, the clatter and clutter. All the multi-tasking challenges like eating and writing and checking email and updating Facebook and drinking coffee and making notes so I don't forget what I want to do next.

You are my hiding place . . .

The words came to me as a whispered invitation, reminding me that I *can* run away— into the waiting, peaceful presence of the Lord.

I can crawl inside His arms, lean my back against His chest, and hide.

Someone once said, "Don't eat lunch at your desk if you can help it."

I add to that, "Sit where you can look outside and see things that are not manmade."

My eyes have never burned and my heart has never ached from looking at God's creation — grass, trees, quail squabbling beneath the birdfeeder. The dog, the cats, a fluffy-cloud sky. Such things soothe me.

Like the small vase of flowers on my desk. They draw my eye to the God-made, the lovely. That which I cannot replicate, though I try to with my words.

Thank You, Father, for knowing what I need most. Thank You for sharing Your presence with me when I desperately need calm and quiet. Amen.

He will cover you with his feathers.
He will shelter you with his wings.
His faithful promises are your armor and protection.

Psalm 91:4

Day Twenty-Four

Cords of Love

I led them with cords of human kindness,
with ties of love. To them I was like
one who lifts a little child to the cheek.

Hosea 11:4 NIV

Mother taught me most of what I know, but four important lessons stand out in my memory—two don'ts and two dos:

Don't . . .

- push your hair behind your ears—it makes them stick out.
- put your hands in your sweater pockets—it makes them sag.

Do . . .

- moisturize your neck as well as your face.
- love Jesus more than anyone, even me.

Mother's advice scored much higher than that of other wisdom merchants in my life with a three-out-of-four for accuracy. Not bad.

The first was probably something she had heard from her mother. The women in our family all have very thick hair, but today we all know that hair isn't what pushes ears in or out.

The second is factual, proven by the old, comfortable sweater I wear around the house but never in public.

The third is a bit of prophetic perception that is better followed than ignored. For as any woman over the age of thirty has discovered, there is no undoing of neglect.

And the fourth is the most precious of all gems Mother could have given me. It is the North Star of her guidance, the essence of what I hope I have instilled in my own children.

Mother was not perfect. Neither am I. We did not see eye to eye on many things. But over the years her words have comforted me—as have God's.

The Lord and I first met through my mother's tender nurturing, and for that introduction I will be forever grateful. For as she taught me to love Him more than anyone else, so I have learned that He loves me more than anyone else ever could.

Thank You, Lord, for my mother's love. I pray for those who did not have such a blessing, that You will make up for that in their lives as only You can do. Amen.

Can a mother forget the baby at her breast
and have no compassion on the child she has borne?
Though she may forget, I will not forget you!
See, I have engraved you on the palms of my hands.

Isaiah 49:15–16 NIV

Day Twenty-Five

The Big W

My God, my God, why have you abandoned me?
Psalm 22:1

Ever feel like it's you against the world—occupationally, relationally, or physically? If it's not one thing, it's another, right? Just when we get our sea legs under us, a rogue wave hits, the deck rolls, and our stomachs follow. Why can't our career, relationships, and health be set on good ol' terra firma?

That little three-letter word, *why*, seems to be the first thing we ask.

When I was a crime-beat reporter for the local newspaper, I covered stories with the five-W approach: Who, What, Where, When, and Why. *Why* was always last in the lineup.

Today, I try to use the same approach when life hits a rough spot for me or someone else. First, I ask not *why*, but *who*?

WHO? Who will I turn to for help? Who is most impacted? Who else is hurting?

Jesus delt with individuals as well as crowds, each in a specific and purposeful way. He listened, wept, shouted, called names. He made promises, made people cry with hope and joy, and made a way for us to reach His Father. Jesus was anything but static.

WHAT? What can I do to survive? What can I do to help? What can I do differently?

At one point, Jesus told people He was the light of the world. Religious leaders didn't like it. He wasn't *what* they had been expecting. You can read the account in John 8:12–20.

WHERE? Where do I go from here? Where can I help? Where is the need?

Jesus revealed His personal stance when addressing adversaries in the John 8 account:

1. I know where I came from (John 8:14).

2. I know where I'm going (John 8:14).

3. I am not alone (John 8:16). In Him, we find origin, destiny, and companionship.

WHEN? When will the pain stop? When can I help?

This might be the most important question. Most of us want what we want right now. Sooner rather than later. Now, or today, is the day of salvation, we read in 2 Corinthians 6:2. We are not promised tomorrow here in this life, but in eternity if we accept His saving grace.

WHY? Why did this happen? Often, we already know. Often, we do not, but "fair" is not part of the answer. Thank God, we don't get what we deserve, but we do get God's help.

HOW? This is often part of the questioning. How can I prevent this from happening again? How can I help those who are hurting? With the Holy Spirit lighting our way, the Lord will direct us. With His strength and protection, we will make it and we can comfort others.

It is not faithless to ask *why*. The psalmist did in Psalm 22, and Jesus did when He cried out from the cross (Mark 15:34). Yet we often snag on that question and it keeps us unbalanced. Focusing on the other questions helps us get our bearings.

Thank You, God, that with You, I can face any upheaval. Please be my purpose, direction, and comfort. Amen.

For God says, "At just the right time, I heard you.
On the day of salvation, I helped you."
Indeed, the "right time" is now.
Today is the day of salvation.

2 Corinthians 6:2

Day Twenty-Six

Living on Pins and Needles

Be anxious for nothing.
Philippians 4:6 NKJV

Every year my little patch of prickly pear cactus blooms with the most delicate yellow flowers—a glaring, gossamer contradiction to the plant's spiny pins growing in protective clusters.

Overshadowing the cactus patch on its east side stands a magnificent Colorado blue spruce with its characteristic blueish-green needles.

This year, the living metaphor captured my attention. Pins and needles, right in my front yard.

To be "on pins and needles" is an idiom that refers to waiting nervously to learn what is going to happen. One can be anxious, in suspense, worried, or excited.

Personally, I don't enjoy living on pins and needles, anxious over what is going to happen next, and I've learned three important facts about this state.

1. This condition has absolutely no productive or positive effect on anything, particularly my health.
2. Ninety-nine percent of all that I've worried about never happened.
3. It is nearly impossible to simply say, "I'm not going to worry about it," whatever *it* may be. I must push the anxiety out of my mind and substitute something else in its place.

God has been aware of these three facts all along, so He tells us how to get away from those pins and needles:

> *Be anxious for nothing, but in everything*
> *by prayer and supplication with thanksgiving,*
> *let your requests be made known to God;*
> *and the peace of God, which surpasses*
> *all understanding, will guard your heart*
> *and minds through Christ Jesus.*
>
> Philippians 4:6-7 NKJV

Did you catch what the replacement is?

Thanksgiving. Telling God all about our worries while thanking Him.

So when we're on pins and needles, what can we thank Him for?

We can thank Him for who He is, what He is, and where He is—which is right in the thick of it with us. And like the beautiful blooming cactus flower, His peace will blossom in our hearts and minds.

We don't have to understand how this works. We just know that it does.

Thank You, God, for working Your miracle of peace in my heart when everything around me is prickly. Help me trust You more and relax in Your presence. Amen.

Peace I leave with you, My peace I give to you;
not as the world gives do I give to you.
Let not your heart be troubled,
neither let it be afraid.

John 14:27 NKJV

Day Twenty-Seven

Washed Up?

He chose his servant David,
calling him from the sheep pens.

Psalm 78:70

Seventeen years ago at a writers' conference in California, I met with a well-known novelist for what industry folk call a "one-on-one." It was the equivalent of a PhD professor sitting down with a kindergartener for a career pep talk.

"What do you write?" the author asked.

I was such a greenhorn that I didn't have a sense of direction other than fiction. As a journalist, I'd covered everything from school board meetings and annual 4-H livestock sales to fatal vehicle accidents and bank robberies. I'd won awards and sold inspirational material to several Christian publications. I knew how to tell a story, but I wanted to start telling my own.

However, I had to pick a category. No novel is for "everybody." Readers choose their favorite genre: historical, romance, suspense, middle grade, mysteries, sci-fi—you get the idea.

I'd taken three partial manuscripts with me to that interview: a children's story, a thirty-day devotional book for women (nonfiction), and a contemporary romantic-suspense novel about a gal in a beach-side bungalow who thought she was being stalked.

What I did not have was focus.

The author looked at one story, handed it back, and eyed me with pity. "It's a little late. You should have started this years ago."

I said thank you and took my thick-skinned reporter's attitude to the next workshop on the conference agenda. That was twenty published novels ago.

I'm grateful that I didn't let that fifteen-minute interview squelch my dream.

Of course, I'm not the only traveler in this world to hit roadblocks.

One of my favorite stories has to do with a young, short-tempered Royal who killed a guy who was mistreating someone else, then ended up a fugitive on the backside of a Middle-Eastern desert herding sheep. He probably thought it was too late, that he'd be a shepherd forever.

God had other plans for Moses.

A teenager named David rocked his way into a king's palace, where he was soon dodging spears, assassination plots, and deadly jealousy.

Then there's Peter, a world-class fisherman who hooked the world with his words because God saw beyond his limitations.

Some of us have old dreams hiding deep inside. Some of us think we're washed up and it's too late because we lost our job, a relationship crumbled, or the doctor gave us bad news.

But here's the news we need to consider: God is never caught by surprise. What we call "too late" could be a reboot.

Jesus said, "Behold, I make all things new" (Revelation 21:5 NKJV).

Like Moses, David, and Peter, let's give Him the chance to do that with our lives.

Thank You, Lord, for Your perfect timing—even when I don't think it is. Amen.

That is why the LORD says, "Turn to me now, while there is time. Give me your hearts."

Joel 2:12

Day Twenty-Eight

Endurance

For you know that when your faith is tested,
your endurance has a chance to grow.

James 1:3

For several years, I awoke to a musical alarm each morning when my bedside radio came on at 5:25. Set to a Christian music station, it played the last five minutes of an inspirational program before the day's non-commercial music began.

Sometimes I crawled out of bed immediately. Sometimes I lay there and listened to the worship. It depended on the day.

Regardless, the radio was programmed to stay on for an hour, a worshipful background to my morning routine. I didn't always actively listen, but it was there, filling my house, filtering down into my spirit, and building me up in the process.

One morning during those first five minutes when I wasn't fully awake, the host quoted James 1:3, though I didn't realize it at the time. I was half asleep and not paying close attention, but what he said sank down into my subconscious without my recognition of it until later.

My morning workout schedule included either a mile-long walk outdoors, which was my preference, or a thirty-minute routine with an exercise coach on TV. That morning, I stayed inside and the exercise routine was exceptionally slow. The coach commented about people not understanding how important a slow workout could be.

"Slow work produces endurance," she said, going on to explain that endurance is long-term strength. Power is immediate strength, as in a sudden burst.

An earlier word from the radio host bobbed to the surface of my mind with brilliant clarity:

"The testing of your faith produces *endurance*."

I was startled by the sudden "newness" of an old concept I'd known about for years. When the exercise coach said power-strength comes from building endurance-strength, everything clicked into place like the tumblers in a safe.

My spiritual tendency is to want power over endurance, because endurance takes time to acquire.

Yes, time. Long-term time. As in perseverance. And it usually requires that four-letter word I'm not fond of—*wait*.

How many times has God encouraged me to slow down and wait? I never realized that He was building enduring strength in me during those hard times of waiting.

Thank You, Lord, for Your patience with me as You build up my spiritual muscles and endurance. Amen.

But those who wait on the LORD
shall renew their strength;
they shall mount up with wings like eagles.
They shall run and not be weary,
they shall walk and not faint.

Isaiah 40:31 NKJV

Day Twenty-Nine

Who Is Your Provider?

My God will meet all your needs
according to the riches of his glory in Christ Jesus.

Philippians 4:19 NIV

One day while working, before the latest wave of technological advancement, I thought I was having problems with my computer. It wasn't doing what I depended on it to do, as in downloading and uploading—things I couldn't explain in techy terms but desperately needed.

Basically, I knew enough to know that I didn't know enough, so I contacted someone who knew more.

"It could be your provider," said the person in the know. "Who is your provider?"

Of course the question referred to my internet service provider, but my attention deviated at that point as I paused for a moment at the sudden fork in the processing path.

Who *is* my provider, in the life sense of the word? Is it me?

Who do I depend on to provide for my needs, safety, and support? Who do I trust with my work and my future? God or myself?

In both technological and spiritual applications, my provider matters—that unseen essence in the background that makes everything work. And the level of my connection to that provider is critical.

The answer to my computer issues that day did lie with my internet service provider. I'd used up all the data or information access I'd paid for and had to buy more. Once that matter was cleared up, everything flowed smoothly.

I'm so glad it's not that way with God, my Life Provider. When there's a glitch in communication with Him, the problem is never on His end. It's always on mine and is usually in one of three areas:

- Do I have a weak connection? (Am I in His Word on a regular basis?)
- Have I substituted other input for His? (Who else am I listening to?)
- Am I depending on myself rather than Him? (Have I put myself in control?)

With God as my Provider, I don't have to worry about "using up" or maxing out His provision. He is ultimately more dependable than anything man has invented and is endlessly limitless in His offer of access.

About two thousand years ago, a rough-cut fisherman named Peter figured this out:

By his divine power, God has given us everything
we need for living a godly life. We have received all of this
by coming to know him, the one who called us to himself
by means of his marvelous glory and excellence.

2 Peter 1:3

Everything we need. That's what I call unlimited access.

Who is your provider?

Heavenly Father, thank You for always being there with Your unlimited power and love. Be my Provider, now and always. Amen.

Since he did not spare even his own Son
but gave him up for us all,
won't he also give us everything else?

Romans 8:32

Day Thirty

Even If

If we are thrown into the blazing furnace,
the God whom we serve is able to save us.

Daniel 3:17 NIV

What would you take with you if you had five minutes to evacuate your home? Many people have had to answer that question.

When I was a newspaper reporter, I covered a lot of bad news and once arrived at a burning house moments before flames burst through the front plate-glass window with a roar.

Thankfully, no one was home. But that family didn't get the chance to choose what they'd save.

I no longer chase down the latest breaking-news story, but I still pay close attention to the fire-ripe conditions in our drought-dry state.

Fires in Colorado and other states are no longer contained to what was once known as "fire season." My heart breaks to hear of homes, livestock, and grazing land consumed by unstoppable, wind-driven flames.

Other natural disasters such as hurricanes, tornadoes, floods, blizzards, and earthquakes leave many people living in fear due to the speed with which they strike.

We have no control over any of them, but we can choose between scared and prepared.

A few years ago when the Royal Gorge Fire threatened our area, my family prepared a grab-and-run plastic tub. It held important files, medications, tech devices, and a few items we wanted to preserve—small things that fit inside and could not be easily replaced.

I was surprised by how many of my possessions *could* be replaced and how many I could live without.

Taking a cue from friends who endured devastating California fires, I backed up my computer off-site. And I took fire-mitigation precautions around the house.

However, the greatest preparation involved my heart. I have no control over anything other than my response. I can choose to live in fear, or I can choose to trust God—even if I have no warning and everything burns up, including the grab-and-run tub.

Even if are pretty big words. The Old Testament prophet, Daniel, wrote of three young Hebrew captives who refused to worship a golden statue set up by the king of Babylon. They insisted that God was able to save them, yet, "Even if he does not . . . we will not serve your gods" (Daniel 3:17–18 NIV).

Today, when the storms and fires come, I am grateful for every hard, frightening, painful time in my life, because they have shown me that I serve a faithful God. I lie down in peace and sleep at night—not because I've cleared dry fuel from around the house or packed up my grab-and-run tub, but because God has gotten me through some serious issues in the past and proven Himself faithful.

He is worthy of my trust. *Even if* everything burns up. *Even if* the results hurt.

Thank you, God, for Your great faithfulness, even if things don't go my way. Amen.

When you go through deep waters, I will be with you.
When you go through rivers of difficulty,
you will not drown. When you walk through the fire
of oppression, you will not be burned up;
the flames will not consume you.

Isaiah 43:2

Day Thirty-One

To Obey or Not to Obey

Obedience is better than sacrifice,
and submission is better than offering the fat of rams.

1 Samuel 15:22

One morning as my old heeler, Blue, and I walked along our country road, I let him off his leash to investigate the rabbit brush and cholla.

Morning has always been my favorite time of day, especially dawn—cool, fresh, full of promise. I try to beat the sunrise so I can watch it peek over the horizon.

That particular morning, danger lurked in the brush. I didn't see it because I was watching the sky for the Canada geese I'd heard calling.

No geese showed, so I turned my attention to Blue, who was riveted on a particular bush along the roadside. His sharp ears pointed straight ahead, and his body braced for attack.

I moved closer, surprised by my old-man heeler who never alerted to much of anything other than squirrels.

That's when I saw it. The locked and loaded black-and-white tail.

"Blue—come!" With as much command as I could muster, I called my near-deaf dog. He didn't move.

Again, "Blue—come!"

After an incredibly long moment, his concentration broke and he glanced my way. I held my breath as he relented and trotted to me.

Blue's obedience saved us both.

With a finger under his collar and a breathy "Good dog," I quickly led him out of range, snapped on his leash, and headed for home. As we rounded the curve in the road, the unmistakable scent of the other critter wafted our way. We had been upwind.

I was knee-quakingly grateful for Blue's obedience. Without it, we could have both been skunked.

All the way home I thought about the ramifications of Blue's obedience and what his failure to do so might have cost us. And I couldn't avoid the quick connection to my own life-choices where obedience to the Lord was involved. My decisions to obey or not have no doubt impacted innocent bystanders, whether family, friends, or onlookers.

We are not the only ones affected by our obedience, either directly or indirectly. The consequences, whether good or bad, waft down into the next generation like perfume on the wind.

God, Your counsel and warnings are all blessings for us when we choose to obey You. Help us listen and obey more and more so it becomes a life-giving habit. Amen.

If you love me, obey my commandments

John 14:15

Day Thirty-Two

Wonder-Speed

Become like little children.
Matthew 18:3 NIV

When my youngest granddaughter was preschool age, we often spent time together discovering the world from her perspective.

One summer day, we watched a hummingbird at the feeder outside the window of my home office. To her, the bird was a marvelous, magical creature that hovered before her unlike anything she had yet seen.

She was fascinated by the movement of the tiny bird's tail.

I understood how it worked, and knew it functioned as a rudder for the bird's aerial acrobatics.

She watched the hummer, captivated by its quick movement because she *didn't* understand how it worked.

Observing it through her inexperienced, four-year-old eyes let me see the winged wonder more clearly and enjoy again the delight of discovery.

Could such an undertone have accompanied the words of Jesus when He said, "Unless you change and become like little children, you will never enter the kingdom of heaven" (Matthew 18:3 NIV)?

I've had to give Jesus's conditional phrase serious thought, for He wasted no words.

I suspect that changing and becoming like a child has to do with unhurried observation, unfaltering faith, and unquestioning joy. Children excel in such innocence. At least until they spend enough time around us hurried, doubt-filled, short-tempered grownups and eventually learn to emulate our behavior.

Can we slow down to wonder-speed, take a closer look, and marvel at God's handiwork—like my husband did the other day.

He took a clementine tangerine outside and sat down in the gazebo swing to enjoy the beautiful day. Easily peeling the seedless citrus, he bit into a juicy section, delighted by its sweet goodness, and praised God for such ingenious creativity.

"Thank you, Lord, for giving us such beautiful and unique things to enjoy. You've created good things for us to eat, sweet to the taste and colorful to the eye."

No, it's not too late for grandparents. Or parents, or adults of any age. Becoming like a child in their simplicity is a choice readily available to us all if we will just slow down to wonder-speed and take a moment to acknowledge God's good gifts.

Maybe then we'll more easily trust Him to lift us on the wings of eagles—and hummingbirds.

Thank You, Lord, for creating such a beautiful world for us to enjoy. Help us see and appreciate the amazing and minuscule things You have made for us, and to praise You with the awe and wonder of a child. Amen.

Let the children come to me. Don't stop them!
For the Kingdom of Heaven belongs to those who are
like these children.

Matthew 19:14

Day Thirty-Three

The Rigors of Rejection

*And we know that God causes everything to work
together for the good of those who love God and
are called according to his purpose for them.*

Romance 8:28

Rejection. We all know what it tastes like—bitter,
regardless of how well-preserved our self-esteem
is.

As a child, I often played the piano for school
talent shows, winning some and losing others.
On those losing occasions, my mother would say,
"You'll always play better than some people but not
as well as others. There is always something else
ahead."

Her wise words lengthened my perspective and helped me bear the bite of childhood
disappointment.

Later rejections included a certain boy in my
high school American History class who never
looked my way and job openings for which I just

knew I was the most qualified. Failure to land a coveted teaching position after college hurt deeply, yet because of that rejection, doors opened that would not have otherwise.

My most stinging rejection was a blow to my career as an author—or so I thought.

A novella manuscript I'd submitted for inclusion in a Christmas collection was turned down by the acquisitions editor. After licking my wounds for a few days, I set to work stretching that storyline into a full-length novel. Another publishing house picked it up and after reading it, offered me a three-book contract for books two and three to follow.

Thrilled, I signed on the dotted line, quivering only slightly since I'd not yet started books two and three. I quickly learned that such a process was common in the publishing industry.

If I had sold the story as a novella, it would have been gone. Instead, it became the seed that grew into my three-book series, The Cañon City Chronicles. That series re-released under a single cover, and I wrote three additional books, turning them all into a six-book series.

All because of an early rejection.

Another of my novels, *An Improper Proposal*, also was rejected early on. Published elsewhere, it has become my best-seller to date and is the first in another three-book series.

Mother was right. Her rendition of Romans 8:28 has carried me through many potholes of rejection over the years, and I expect it will see me through others yet to come.

It's easy to forget that God has a way of working everything out for our good. He is the Great Recycler of Human Wreckage and encourages us not to allow the rigors of rejection to become rigor mortis.

Thank You, Lord, for Your ongoing encouragement to not give up on the gifts You have given me. Thank You for helping me learn and grow and improve for Your glory. Amen.

I press on toward the goal to win the prize for which God has called me heavenward in Christ Jesus.

Philippians 3:14 NIV

Day Thirty-Four

Choose Joy

The joy of the LORD is your strength.
Nehemiah 8:10 NIV

I received a note from a friend the other day. Part of it said, "Surround yourself with what you love."

Sometimes I do this without thinking about it, haphazardly scattering colors or keepsakes that appeal to me. Without serious consideration, I simply like the feel or look of certain things.

At other times, I deliberately choose the imagery and symbolism of my environment because of how it speaks to me. During particularly hard days, these choices become more important, and I find myself looking purposefully for that which stirs joy.

Why make such a big deal out of it?

Because everything speaks to us whether we are actively listening or not, and much of what our world has to say is deceptive and depressing.

In our easily connected, technological age, we daily receive countless messages. These messages can be overwhelming—from news of natural disasters and crumbling governments, infrastructures, and families, to cynicism of the media and subtle references to an inactive, disinterested God. After a while, I'm depressed and discouraged and wondering why.

So I have decided to surround myself with what is uplifting. For me, this involves active choices of the music I listen to, the books I read, the movies I watch, and even the amount of news I ingest. It all affects me to some degree.

Since there is so very much *non*joy in the world, I choose joy and the things that bring it.

Not long ago, I watched a movie during which an adult daughter brought her mother a flowering, potted plant. The mother said, "Flowers die. They're a waste of money."

What died was a little piece of the daughter who made the overture.

Yes, flowers die. So will we. Does that mean we quit living?

Flowers may not appeal to everyone, but they do to many. Depending on their form, they can evoke a sense of cheerfulness or celebration. Even if only for a moment, they have the power to uplift and encourage.

Why do you suppose God made flowers of such varied color and fragrance? And what about food? Why so many different types with such rich flavors and textures?

The same observation can be made of trees, wildlife, even geological formations. The point is creation could have been purely functional. Instead, it's filled with beauty and blessing, reflecting who God is. It reveals His love and care, the delight and joy of His presence.

Within the freewill we've been given lies everyday choices of simple preferences. Choose joy!

Thank You, our most gracious God, for delighting in creation and sharing the joy of Your heart with us. Amen.

You will show me the path of life;
in Your presence is fullness of joy;
at Your right hand are pleasures forevermore.
Psalm 16:11 NKJV

Day Thirty-Five

Storing the Light

Arise, shine, for your light has come.
Isaiah 60:1 NIV

Solar lights mark the juncture of my driveway with the main road. On sunny days, they collect enough energy to cast a soft glow after dark, lighting the entrance to our drive. I never have to turn them on, and they cost me nothing to operate. They are always storing the light.

Unless the weather plays against me.

On cloudy days, the tiny solar cells collect no energy and have nothing to share in the dark that evening.

I operate in much the same way. Some days I'm bright and shiny; on others I'm dull and gloomy. It all depends on what I've been collecting.

Unlike our solar lights, God's light is indifferent to the weather. It doesn't matter if emotional storms cloud my heart; His stores of truth and wisdom remain inexhaustible. The more I have on reserve, the brighter my own light shines. But if I'm too busy, anxious, or depressed to soak up the hope and comfort of His Word, darkness washes in around me.

Darkness is manifested in different ways but is constant in its makeup: it is the *absence* of light. That's why it cannot overwhelm or dominate light, no matter how small that light may be. Even a tiny flicker glows bravely against the blackest void.

Scripture tells us that there is no darkness in God—no absence of light—for He *is* light.

God's first choice of creative expression was light. He spoke it, and it became. Read the Genesis account of creation and note that light appeared three days before God set the sun and moon upon their courses and flung the stars into space.

Light shines throughout all the Scripture, glittering from the face of Moses, pulsing through the visions of Isaiah, and blinding the eyes of a fervent fanatic named Paul who gained more than his sight when he opened his heart.

Jesus said, "I am the light of the world" (John 8:12 NIV). When Light took life by the hand and stepped into our world, color and warmth weren't far behind.

Let's recharge our soul-cells with the Son-Light of God by opening His word and filling ourselves with His life-giving light.

May His light shine from us. When we are backed against the wall and squeezed, may His radiance leak out through the cracks in our lives.

Thank You, Lord of Life and Light, for giving us Your Holy Spirit so we can shine with Your light, spreading hope to those around us. Amen.

*This is the message we heard from Jesus
and now declare to you: God is light,
and there is no darkness in him at all.*

1 John 1:5

Day Thirty-Six

Who's Your Wagon Master?

I am the light of the world. If you follow me,
you won't have to walk in darkness,
because you will have the light that leads to life.

John 8:12

One of my favorite paintings is *The Wagon Master,* a 1909 oil by C.M. Russell. A print of it hangs in my living room, and every time I consider the story that Charles Russell is portraying, I am reminded of two important choices we make in life: leadership and community.

The painting depicts an 1800s wagon *train pulled by oxen and* heading west after crossing a river. Trains were more likely to make the cross-continent trip than lone wagons in those early expansion days, and travelers relied heavily upon the principle of safety in numbers.

Russell's wagon master is prepared with an attentive horse, a rifle, a knife, spurs, and a bull whip looped over his shoulder. His neckerchief, wide-brim hat, and leggings aren't for show. Each serves a purpose.

Ahead of the slow-moving train, he looks back, watching it climb out of a river valley. A rattler watches him from the scrub brush, and deep ruts in the prairie ahead bear witness to trains that traveled this way before.

The wagon master had to know where the train was headed and the safest route. The best leaders had been to the desired destination and back at least once, so they knew the dangers and risks, as well as vital sources of forage and water. Stories have been told of those who did not fit the criteria, and peril was the result of their efforts. The wagon master carried tremendous responsibility for the lives of those in his train and had to be bold enough to make unpopular decisions.

The train was a temporary neighborhood comprised of people with a common goal—a tight-knit community for the long months required to make the arduous journey. Not every sojourner made it to their destination, and many were buried along the trail, including infants. But those who grieved loss did not grieve alone. Members of a wagon train helped each other with support and encouragement, even food and supplies when necessary.

"Circle the wagons" meant to prepare for attack. A circle formation of large, canvas-covered farm or freight wagons created a barrier between people and animals inside the ring and invaders and scavengers outside of it. Still today, its metaphorical usage is clearly understood.

As good artwork does, Russell's print speaks to my heart, as if asking, "Do you have community? Do you have leadership?"

By God's grace, I can say yes to both questions.

Like the westward journey, life often presents danger and discouragement. I draw comfort and comradery from a community of believers who share my faith, and I measure our leadership's qualifications against the written words of God.

Jesus is my ultimate leader, but He provides community in fellowship with others who follow him. If you've not yet found community and leadership in this transient life, ask the Lord to show you, and be willing to join the train.

Seek his will in all you do,
and he will show you which path to take.

Proverbs 3:6

Day Thirty-Seven

Hurry, Hurry, Hurry

My days are swifter than a runner.

Job 9:25 NIV

One morning as I hurried around the house, fretting over my growing to-do list, I muttered, "Did time go this fast for the Hebrews who wandered in the wilderness? Or when David was a shepherd boy? Or when Jesus walked on earth as a man? Did it fly then like it does for me now, Lord?"

Already the month was more than half over! Where had the days gone?

A few moments after indulging in that glass of *whine*, I sat down with my copy of *Daily Light*, a collection of topical Scriptures compiled in the late 1800s. Turning to the day's page, I read Job 9:25.

Wow. Clearly, my complaint was not original if a man who'd lived thousands of years before felt the same way.

Not long after my revelation with *Daily Light*, my son texted me a screenshot of his smartphone timer. He often joked about spending an inordinate amount of time waiting in checkout lines at a local store. To prove the lengthy wait at this particular store, he set the stopwatch on his phone during that day's visit, confident it would register at least a half hour.

The screenshot revealed the actual amount of time used, beginning from when he entered the line behind two other shoppers with full carts, checked out, walked to his car, unloaded his purchases, took his cart to the cart corral, walked back to his car, got in, and started the engine.

Just over eight minutes.

"We're living too fast," he texted after sending me the photo.

My son recognized the inward push that makes him hurry and miss out on interacting with the people and environment around him.

Job 29:25–26 describes Job's lament more fully:

"My days are swifter than a runner; they fly away without a glimpse of joy. They skim past like boats of papyrus, like eagles swooping down on their prey" (NIV).

I cannot agree with Job in his joylessness, for I am surrounded by God's innumerable blessings. They are everywhere, obvious and hidden, small and great, exuberant and serene.

But they will pass me in a whir if I don't slow down and listen, observe, touch, taste, and smell them.

Time is as God set it in the beginning—the same. The problem is my perception and application of it.

Lord, please show me what I can do this week to slow down and catch a glimpse of Your blessings all around me. Amen.

Enthusiasm without knowledge is no good;
haste makes mistakes.

Proverbs 19:2

Day Thirty-Eight

Going Off-Grid

After he had dismissed them, he went up on a mountainside by himself to pray.

Matthew 14:23 NIV

Last month I left everything behind and went off-grid.

Well, sort of.

I took my laptop because I was going to write. Which meant I also needed my smart phone and Nikon camera. Now that I think about it, I didn't leave *everything* behind after all.

"Off-grid" is more of a disconnect-descriptor for those who choose to live more independently without cultural infrastructure such as electricity, etc. For me, "off-grid" simply meant "out of reach."

I needed the getaway. Sweet evenings by a whispering river with no television or phone calls or internet. Oh, there was Wi-Fi, but there was also an off/mute button, complete with the rebellious sense of, "I'm gone, and no one knows where I am."

True off-gridders would have camped. I did the next best thing at a mountain-valley Airbnb with gracious hosts and a guardian feline that kept a careful but distant eye on me from beneath a flowering tree in the yard.

I wonder if Jesus felt like that when He went off by Himself to pray.

As much as I enjoyed those few days alone, I had to leave. But I've learned that leaving means taking parts of my retreat home with me—like the sweet aftertaste of waking to a quiet dawn and walking by the river. Goslings in the pasture, the swaying music of giant cottonwoods, sunlight gilding not-so-distant snow-capped peaks.

Somehow, going off-grid made coming back easier. I think it's because I came back with the peace of "away."

The anticipation of leaving and enjoyment of the experience, and remembering the change of pace, place, and priority all wove into the regeneration I needed.

He restores my soul.

If I let Him.

For me, renewal requires simpler over easier/faster. Convenience can be an emotionally costly commodity.

How about you? How do you regenerate? Do you go "off-grid"?

If you could go away for a few days, where would you go—mountains, desert, seashore, or somewhere else?

_____

_____

_____

_____

Thank You, Lord, for the example You set for us when You sought solitude. We need it to fully function. Help us follow Your example. Amen.

Peter went up on the roof to pray.

Acts 10:9 NIV

Day Thirty-Nine

How's Your Curb Appeal?

*In the same way, let your light shine before others,
that they may see your good deeds
and glorify your Father in heaven.*

Matthew 5:16 NIV

Sometimes we no longer see the things we've grown accustomed to.

Such an observation works for the bad as well as the good.

One summer I revamped the front of my house by removing an old, dry cedar hedge. If I had known its removal would make such a drastic difference, I would have done it years before.

But I'd gotten used to seeing it, so I didn't really *see* it.

Nor did I see the two twenty-year-old spruce trees behind the hedge. Yes, they were taller, but the ugly hedge drew my attention, not the magnificent evergreens.

I didn't eliminate the thirty-foot long hedge without help. I could have chipped away at it a piece at a time, but getting qualified people with the skills and necessary equipment to do the job was worth every penny spent and every ounce of frustration saved.

Since the big change, I've wondered if this elimination process applies to my personality or my spiritual life. How's my curb appeal? Is there a habit in my life that blocks people's view of Jesus? What ugly irritant in my disposition draws their attention away from lovelier aspects? What do I need to have removed?

When I got rid of the ugly hedge, I saw the regal beauty of the spruce trees.

As a Christ-follower, my curb appeal is important. Not as a façade covering an unlovely building, but as an attraction to those who need the transforming grace of Jesus in their lives. Is there something that needs to be removed so others can see the real me?

If you sense the need for an update in your life, seek help from people with the right skills and tools. Ask God to lead you to them and trust that He will.

Lord, please show me myself as You see me—warts and all. I know You love me unconditionally, but please change what does not reflect positively on You. Only You can make the transformation in my life. Amen.

Therefore, as God's chosen people, holy and dearly loved, clothe yourselves with compassion, kindness, humility, gentleness and patience.

Colossians 3:12 NIV

Day Forty

The Unseen Landscape

He counts the stars and calls them all by name.

Psalm 147:4

I couldn't sleep. The four o'clock hour winked in digital red from my clock radio, so I went to the living room and opened the windows and door, welcoming the coolness of predawn.

At the door, I stilled. For there in the night sky rose one of the few constellations I can identify— Orion—clear and shining against the black canopy. Some civilizations have called him "The Hunter," rising above the treetops with his sword and club.

I am not a student of the stars. I am, however, a student of the Star-Maker, and I recognized His handiwork, flung – the scriptures say – from His fingertips.

Recorded in the oldest of the biblical books is God's conversation with a man named Job. A man who, I imagine, viewed many a night sky unpolluted by artificial light. How brilliantly it must have glittered then!

"Can you bind the cluster of the Pleiades, or loose the belt of Orion?" God asked him (see Job 38:31).

How small Job must have felt.

How small I felt when, an hour later, Orion was gone, having paled against the approaching dawn. Yet I had a sense he was still there, striding the heavens.

He was certainly there, as are all the celestial lights, though diminished in daylight by the sun. The sky holds an unseen landscape that we forget about as we go about our daily business.

I have since wondered why I saw Orion during his brief appearance that early morning. Was it one of God's ways of reminding me of His presence even though I don't see Him?

It is in God's nature to comfort His people with His closeness, as when he opened the eyes of the prophet Elisha's servant to see the unseen army protecting them from an approaching enemy.

"Do not fear, for those who are with us are more than those who are with them," Elisha told the frightened young man. The Lord allowed the servant to see "the hills full of horses and chariots of fire all around Elisha" (2 Kings 6:17 NIV).

I may not always sense the Lord of Heaven's Armies by my side, but I appreciate His reminders—in whatever form they may come. For in my journey on this earth, I am still learning to "not look at the things which are seen, but at the things which are not seen" (2 Corinthians 4:17–18 NKJV).

Thank You, Lord, for the brilliance of the night sky and the knowledge that even when we can't see them, the stars and planets still hang above us. Thank You for Your abiding presence that is even more certain than the lights of Your creation. Amen.

He alone has spread out the heavens
And marches on the waves of the sea.
He made all the stars—the Bear and Orion, the Pleiades
and the constellations of the southern sky.

Job 9:8-9

Day Forty-One

My Name Is Written

Rejoice that your names are written in heaven.
Luke 10:20 NIV

A child's perspective can open our eyes to things we've forgotten about as adults.

Like the vintage carnival-prize horse that belonged to my mother-in-law. Her great-granddaughter discovered that prize several months ago and let me know that she placed high value upon it. She picked it up, turned it over and around, and even hugged it to her little chest in adoration.

One day when she was visiting, she went predictably to the little horse and picked it up, surprised by the piece of paper taped to its copper belly.

"That's your name on there," I said when she looked to me for explanation. "Someday, that horse will be yours."

Again, she hugged it endearingly.

Falling in love with horses is a common malady among young girls, and it often hangs around through adulthood. I suffered from it myself and was never quite cured.

A friend of mine told me that some people simply have a horseshoe-shaped link in their DNA. I think she's right.

Each time my granddaughter visits, she checks the carnival horse. "My name is on it," she says. "And tape."

She's reminding me of her future ownership as well as reassuring herself that I won't forget. Though she doesn't know it, she is also reminding me of God's unfailing love for us as His children.

The Old Testament prophet Isaiah encouraged the people with God's words. "Can a mother forget the baby at her breast and have no compassion on the child she has borne? Though she may forget, I will not forget you! See, I have engraved you on the palms of my hands;" (Isaiah 49:15–16 NIV).

In the New Testament, Jesus told His disciples upon their return from seeing evil succumb to God's power, "Don't rejoice that the spirits submit to you, rejoice that your names are written in heaven" (Luke 10:20 NIV).

Written in heaven. I like the sound of that. There is great comfort in knowing that my name is written there, much more indelibly than ink on a piece of tape.

Thank You, Lord, for allowing us to see You through the eyes of a child. And thank You that in Your eyes, we will always be Your children. Amen.

Nothing evil will be allowed to enter,
not anyone who practices shameful idolatry
and dishonesty—but only those whose names
are written in the Lamb's Book of Life.

Revelation 21:27

Day Forty-Two

You Are of More Value

Do not fear therefore;
you are of more value than many sparrows.

Matthew 10:31 NKJV

What was that hanging from my bird feeder—a bat?

I looked again. Sparrows swarmed the feeder and the ground beneath it, scrabbling for seeds and corn in the snow.

The dangling creature flapped its wings and tried to upright itself, and I saw what it was. A bird. A tiny sparrow.

Again it fell and hung by one foot snared in the feeder's decorative edging. I'd never seen such a thing.

Pulling on my snow boots and gloves, I briefly regretted the disturbance my presence would cause the other birds, particularly the covey of quail huddled nearby beneath a sheltering spruce. But I could not let the single bird hang there until it froze to death or was snagged by a hawk.

As I approached, the other birds scattered in a rush of wings. Only the captive remained, flailing and chirping, possibly in panic. Gray and plain, she lacked the bold markings of the more colorful males. Her little eyes watched me as she cried, but she was no match for my gloved fingers that cupped her wings close to her body.

The bones of her foot were thinner than the smallest twig. I reached beneath the rim of the feeder, hoping to dislodge her foot from the other side without snapping her leg in two.

It worked.

Once clear of the ornate prison, I opened my hand that held her, and she flew away to feed again.

I'd done something right.

I thought of the shepherd who left a flock of ninety-nine sheep to rescue the one that was missing. Though the metaphor clashes with Jesus's words about our value compared to sparrows, both stories speak to how much He loves us. How He has gone out of His way to show us that love and to rescue us.

Inside, I pulled off my boots and stood at the window watching the sparrows return to their feeding ground, seemingly unconcerned that one of their own had been at risk and was rescued, and unaware of the daily delight I took in watching them and feeding them.

May we never forget how precious we are to the One who watches over us and provides for our every need.

Thank You, faithful Father, for seeing our every move and coming to our rescue. Amen.

Are not two sparrows sold for a penny?
Yet not one of them will fall to the ground
outside your Father's care.

Matthew 10:29 NIV

Day Forty-Three

Preparing for Me

I go to prepare a place for you.
John 14:2 NKJV

How many of us today prepare meals? I can think of a few people who go all out when it comes to cooking and inviting, or putting on a big spread, as ranch families might say.

But we have busy lives, right? Times have not only changed, they have diminished. Too often we simply open a box or a pull-top can and call it good.

However, not everyone cuts back on their cooking because of time constraints. Single people rarely serve themselves full-fledged meals at all—like my mother who quit fixing supper after Dad passed. Why bother if you can't prepare something for the one you love?

I think that's the connection. Love.

Jesus spent time eating with people: at the wedding in Canaan, at the tax collector's house, at Lazarus's home.

Scripture contains many references to tables and meals, from the Passover seder to the Marriage Supper of the Lamb. Some of Jesus's parables touch on food, such as the story of the wealthy man to whose lavish meal no invited guests would come (Luke 14:15–23). Or the father's celebratory feast when his prodigal son returned home (Luke 15:11–24).

One day, Jesus told a despised tax collector, Zacchaeus, that He would be eating at his house (Luke 19:1–10). This sent the religious leaders into an uproar, for they considered tax collectors unacceptable. But when He shared a meal with them, they heard what He thought of their pious self-opinions (Luke 11:37–54).

One of Jesus's most repeated sayings is found in the book of Revelation: "I stand at the door and knock. If anyone hears my voice and opens the door, I will come in and eat with that person, and they with me" (Revelation 3:20 NIV). This suggests a personal encounter.

So what's the big deal about sharing a meal with others? As mentioned earlier, it has to do with love. A certain level of intimacy accompanies those who gather around a common table, facing each other, sharing food as well as thoughts and feelings.

It has to do with the extra effort inherent in preparation—even if that preparation is opening the pizza box and passing out napkins.

When Jesus said He was going to prepare a place for us, He wasn't talking only about a place setting at a table, but an eternal home with Him. When I think about Him preparing something for me, it makes me feel loved. I believe that was His intention.

The next time you sit down for a meal with others, whether family, friends, or newcomers, turn off the television and cell phones and face them. Make them feel welcomed and worthy by sharing your food and laughter, and simply enjoy their presence.

Look at and listen to those around you. Share more than a meal—share your heart.

Thank You, Lord, for inviting us to dine with You, whether at a meal of grilled fish on the seashore or a banquet fit for You, our King. Amen.

Salvation has come to this home today.

Luke 19:9

Day Forty-Four

Power Source

Be strong in the Lord and in His mighty power.
Ephesians 6:10 NIV

One evening last winter, the power went out in my neck of the woods. Thankfully, the outside temperature had warmed up to a balmy thirty degrees.

I was already wrapped up in a quilt in my rocker, writing on my laptop, so it wasn't the end of my make-believe world or my real one either. I had plenty of wood stacked on the hearth and a campfire coffee pot full of water on the wood stove in case hot cocoa crossed my mind.

If the outage lasted through the night, I had kerosene lamps and plenty of quilts for sleeping by the fire so I could keep it going all night.

I can do this, I thought. *I write books about people who live without electricity—I know how this works.*

An odd sense of adventure set in and my situation became cozy rather than inconvenient.

A whole forty-five minutes later when the power kicked on, I was almost disappointed. Almost.

But just in case it kicked off again, I started a big kettle of soup and made a batch of biscuits. I could heat up both of them on the wood stove later if necessary. And I knew a lady who had lived in Alaska almost forever, so I could always ask her a few questions.

Oh, how dependent I was on my power sources, whether electrical, gas, propane, solar, or good ol' firelight.

The situation made me consider my life power source. The One who keeps the light on in my soul. He doesn't flicker with rolling blackouts or cut back on energy to save money. He doesn't get knocked out by the wind.

He's always there. Always faithful. Always watching out for us.

Anxiety pales in the glow of such all-powerful faithfulness.

God's got this. Whatever it is.

When the metaphorical lights go out—and they will—who or what will be your power source?

Thank You, Lord, that Your light shines in the darkness and the darkness will never be able to knock it out. Amen.

We also pray that you will be strengthened with all his glorious power so you will have all the endurance and patience you need.

Colossians 1:11

Day Forty-Five

Good Doesn't Mean Easy

For the joy set before him he endured the cross,
scorning its shame,
and sat down at the right hand of the throne of God.

Hebrews 12:2 NIV

"It's a difficult journey, to be sure," my friend said. "But a good one."

My friend was right.

She had been on the journey with me for several years and understood the dark places and sudden drop-offs. The unexpected bends and endless monotony. The oh-so-very-hard times that always broke out into God's faithfulness.

I wrote a book during this journey and the process was difficult. In fact, I stopped halfway through and started over from the beginning.

Maybe the agony of those days came through the story of two people with wounds and scars and doubts about God and forgiveness.

I wonder, because readers shared bits of themselves when telling me how they responded to the book. They pointed out moments in the story that touched their hearts or drew laughter and understanding—or how it made them cry or cheer. They shared things with me that made me believe we were on the journey together even if we didn't know each other.

I continue to be amazed at how God works things out in my life—things that might not necessarily be pleasant or easy. But He works them out for good. Some way, somehow, He always does that. And it makes the suffering worth it.

(Did I really just say it makes the suffering worth it?)

Let me take a deep breath and count to ten . . .

Yes. It's true.

Because His faithfulness is faultless.

His love is relentless.

His comfort and presence priceless.

The "rough patch" in the road is never easy. It hurts. It forces me to live day by day. Makes me look at only today and find the joy in it, regardless how small. Find something to praise Him for even if it's just my morning coffee. Or the coffee cup.

I'm learning that I have no control over anything other than my heart. So I live moment by moment. I stay out of the future. I've grieved. I've buried. I've come full circle. My mind wants to move on. But I'm forced to live in . . .

The. Right. Now.

I'm learning to enjoy this so-very-different time. To enjoy Him.

Thank You, God—yes, thank You for this very-different gift. Thank You for guiding me through each sharp turn. Thank You for showing me the simplicity of "right now" and resting in You. Amen.

But he said to me, "My grace is sufficient for you, for my power is made perfect in weakness."

2 Corinthians 12:9 NIV

Day Forty-Six

Know the Truth, Catch the Lie

I am the way, the truth, and the life.

John 14:6

In a recent Bible-study discussion on the inward change of a person's nature, the participants were directed to 2 Corinthians 3:18 (NKJV):

But we all, with unveiled face,
beholding as in a mirror the glory of the Lord,
are being transformed into the same image
from glory to glory,
just as by the Spirit of the Lord.

This passage tells us that we are changed by looking at the Lord and focusing on Him. As we do our part of "beholding" Jesus, God's Spirit works the miracle of change in us.

But how do we know if we're looking at the real image rather than a knock-off copy or cheap imitation?

The same way bank tellers know when counterfeit bills come through their window.

Tellers are trained in their line of work to distinguish between authentic bills and those that are fake. I've heard that they learn to detect the difference by handling real money. They look at and handle *only* the real deal. Thus, their familiarity with the authentic alerts them to the counterfeit.

The illustration came full circle for me when one of the recent Bible-study participants turned out to be a former bank teller who confirmed what I had heard.

By handling the truth, a teller catches the lie when it comes across the counter, she said. They don't even have to look at the counterfeit. They can feel it.

Can we say then, that on a spiritual level, we become like that upon which we focus?

By learning about Christ Jesus as presented in the Word of God, we become familiar with the truth. When we become so familiar with our Lord by spending time in His Word and in prayer, listening for His voice, we will more easily detect counterfeit "truths" offered by the world. Our part is to make an effort to learn the Lord. His part is to make the change in us by His Holy Spirit.

Oh, God of all creation, thank You for Your unique and perfect Self. Thank You for helping us become more like You as we spend time with You. Help us to do that more and more. Amen.

Put on your new nature, and be renewed as you learn to know your Creator and become like him.

Colossians 3:10

Day Forty-Seven

Exercise Your Free Will

A mocker resents correction;
he will not consult the wise.

Proverbs 15:12 NIV

Every time I pull up to the stop light at the railroad junction in town, I exercise my free will by complying with what the sign says:

"Do not stop on tracks."

The latent twelve-year-old inside my head always chirps, "Duh!"

However, I see people stop on the tracks all the time.

The first vehicle to arrive at the light has room to stop on the other side of the tracks before the intersection of a state highway. The second vehicle might be able to squeeze in behind the first, but the third will be squarely on the tracks, followed by a line of eager motorists waiting for the light to change.

The road is four lanes with automatic barricades on both sides of the tracks. When a train comes, barricade arms lower across the road on each side. If a car is waiting on the tracks, it is boxed in by other vehicles as well as the barricade. I don't want to be in the car that is stuck on the tracks, unable to escape.

Neither do I want the sign above my plot at the cemetery to say "Chose Poorly."

Simply put, there is protection in obedience. Yet how many times do our independence-hackles rise against such wisdom? We don't like the word *obedience* because we want to make our own choices and we *don't* want somebody else to tell us what to do.

God in His creative love and wisdom has given us free will. He's also given us advice regarding what works and what doesn't when it comes to living on this beautiful earth. We can exercise our free will by taking His advice or not.

At various times, we all ignore His advice.

God does not force us to obey, He gives us the freedom of choice. But choices come with consequences and they are pretty well locked in. Like the car on the tracks whose driver chooses to disregard the warning.

The fifteenth chapter of the book of Proverbs has a great deal to say about correction, discipline, prudence, wisdom, and other outdated words, particularly verses 5–12. In fact, the whole book is full of witty sayings about wisdom and choices.

Let's exercise our free will by listening to what God has to say about life and making wise choices.

Thank You, Lord, for showing us how we are protected in obedience. Help us heed Your Word and warnings and reap the benefits of obeying You. Amen.

But if serving the LORD seems undesirable to you,
then choose for yourselves this day whom
you will serve . . .. But as for me and my household,
we will serve the LORD.

Joshua 24:15 NIV

Day Forty-Eight

My Constant Comment

Everyone should be quick to listen,
slow to speak and slow to become angry.

James 1:19 NIV

In my early twenties, I worked briefly for an insurance company in a small northern Colorado farming community. During my lunch break, I often walked the length of the shady street where the office was located. At one corner stood a beautifully maintained Victorian home surrounded by well-kept lawns and sidewalks. An older woman with a white topknot in the style of Katharine Hepburn swept her sidewalk every day.

Her name was Abbie Winnie.

Abbie Winnie and I became friends. She invited me to her upstairs apartment in the old Victorian and introduced me to Constant Comment tea—an acquaintance I had not yet made.

Abbie's cozy apartment was furnished from bygone years with things she loved, including a small black-and-white framed picture of herself as a child and one of her son. I learned that he looked nothing like the image that sat atop an antique bureau in the tiny living room, for during the Second World War he underwent plastic surgery that altered his facial features so he could more easily infiltrate enemy territory.

She didn't know exactly what he had done during his military service. He never told her.

Abbie Winnie has passed from my life, but over the years Constant Comment has become one of my favorite teas. Each time I tear open the red-and-black seal, I think of the vibrant little white-haired woman and our "May–December" friendship.

Curiosity prompted me to research the tea, and I learned that Constant Comment received its unusual name from its creator, Ruth Campbell Bigelow, who said her friends constantly commented on their enjoyment of the spicy-citrus blend.

However, the name always leads me to consider my own comments—over tea and otherwise. Am I constantly commenting? Jabbering away without listening to what others may have to say.

I hope not.

Abbie Winnie taught me a great deal about friendship all those years ago, and I pray that I will continue to listen more than I speak and learn more than I share.

Thank You, Lord, for the people You bring into our lives with messages of friendship and love. You have hand-picked them for each of us in particular. Thank You for knowing us that well. Amen.

The heart of the godly thinks carefully before speaking.

Proverbs. 15:28

Day Forty-Nine

The Little Things

Catch for us the foxes, the little foxes
that ruin the vineyards.

Song of Solomon 2:15 NIV

It's the little things that make me lose my mind—my patience, my cool, my grip on appropriate vocabulary in the English language.

One of those little things is a nut. Not a tree nut, but the small, grooved fastener that holds a bolt in place on the bracket that holds the axle that holds the wheel that provides mobility for my wheelbarrow.

Yes, that nut.

When I have a load of firewood and one of those nuts unscrews itself and falls off where I will never find it, the axle slips, the wheel drops, and the load dumps right there wherever I am, which is never where I want to end up.

It happened three times last week.

A neighbor tightened the nuts for me, much tighter than I could get them myself. Problem solved. (Problem solved even further by using lock nuts.)

However, it's also the little things that make a huge difference in life. Take the house key, for example. A two-inch-long piece of metal gives me access to my home. Without it, I'd be breaking a window to get inside.

Most of the time, I take the little things in my life for granted. I overlook their importance, simply counting on them to be there when I need them.

But if I neglect them, they are *not* there when I need them.

One of the most important "little things" in my life is the time I spend in the mornings with the Lord. I'm a forgetful human who often springs emotional leaks. I need an ongoing source of strength that keeps my wheels on and opens the door to peace that sees me through chaotic times.

An anonymous proverb quoted in variation over the centuries makes the point quite clear:

For want of a nail the shoe was lost.
For want of a shoe the horse was lost.
For want of a horse the rider was lost.
For want of a rider the battle was lost.

For want of a battle the kingdom was lost.
And all for the want of a horseshoe nail.

What little things in your life have you been neglecting that could make a huge difference in how things go?

I'm grateful, Lord, that it is You who holds our wheels on and helps us keep our emotions in check. Thank You for providing the peace that sees us through chaotic times. Amen.

The tongue is a small part of the body,
but it makes great boasts. Consider what a great forest
is set on fire by a small spark.

James 3:5 NIV

Day Fifty

He Knows Us

*O LORD, you have examined my heart
and know everything about me.*

Psalm 139:1

"I talk about these made-up people as if they were real. I know them better than most actual people."

Over coffee, a friend and I were discussing the characters in my recently released novel.

She looked at me as if I'd just made the most perfectly normal comment. "That's because you know their hearts," she said. "You created them. That's how God knows us."

I'd never thought about it like that before. She was right.

I knew Ella Canaday and Cale Hutton[1] and would recognize them on the street. Ella had a deep heart-wound that overshadowed her physical disability. Cale worked hard to hide his loneliness.

---

[1] Davalynn Spencer, *A Change of Scenery* (Colorado: Wilson Creek Publishing, 2021).

I knew they could help each other if they could just get past all the pretense, misconceptions, and self-erected barriers.

As my friend said, that's how God knows us.

He also knows that obstacles help create growth—if we don't opt for quitting first.

Isn't that the way it is in real life? We run up against conflict and insurmountable odds all the time. We either back down or press on. And that choice makes a difference in who we become.

God knows our odds and obstacles. He knows us more intimately than we could ever imagine. He knows what makes us tick—what makes us laugh, growl, cry—and why. Yet He loves us beyond our highest hopes and most desperate dreams.

That's incredible love.

Lord, help me recognize the way You work in my heart and life to grow me into the person You want me to be. Amen.

Consider it pure joy, my brothers and sisters,
whenever you face trials of many kinds,
because you know that the testing of your
faith produces perseverance.

Let perseverance finish its work so that you may be mature and complete, not lacking anything.

James 1:3–4 NIV

Day Fifty-One

Over-Firing

It is useless for you to work so hard
from early morning until late at night,
anxiously working for food to eat;
for God gives rest to his loved ones.

Psalm 27:2

When we moved into a new-to-us home one fall, I was thrilled with its little wood stove. I wanted to be ready for action *before* the first snow of the season, so I read up on its operations, noting the warning label on the footing: "If unit or chimney connector glows you are over-firing."

No kidding.

In small print below the obvious disclaimer it said "Type of fuel: wood only."

I asked a local stove company employee about that, and she said the stove was not approved for burning coal, which burns much hotter than wood. I wondered if anyone had ever "over fired" their stove to the glowing point, thus prompting the printed warning.

As a wife/author/musician/speaker/grand-mother, I often over-fired and glowed because of it all. Not the welcoming glow that draws weary travelers to a warm hearth, but a raging burnout that threatened to shoot the chimney off the roof. This was usually the result of my inability to say no—the equivalent of filling a wood-only firebox with chunks of coal and letting time constraints fan the flame.

Eventually, I understood the Lord's warning that just because I *could* do something didn't mean I *should*. And just because a project was worthy of my time and effort didn't mean I had to join the process. Learning to say no was easier when I focused on the following three steps:

- Prioritize: Prioritizing required me to first check with the Lord. What did He want me to write/do/give? Did His assignment earn the "first fruits" of my time and creative process? Or did I try to clear away the virtual clutter first, and then approach my true calling with the dregs of left-over energy?

- Energize: As a grownup, I knew how to eat well, but I didn't always follow through. Chocolate is a vegetable, right? Wait—cocoa beans grow on the cacao tree, so maybe it's fruit. Okay, okay. There was probably a better snack than a bag of chocolate chips.
- Realize: I believed Psalm 46:10 was telling me to get a clue and *realize* who was in control. I had discovered (along with Mark Twain) that all the problems I worried about never happened. Unless I used those problems in my next plot line, worrying about them was a total waste of time.

That winter, my woodstove helped me remember to Prioritize, Energize, and Realize. If I didn't feed myself unnecessary projects, I did more by doing less and didn't over fire in the process.

Thank You, Lord, for speaking to me in unexpected but oh-so-perfect ways. Amen.

Don't worry about anything;
instead, pray about everything.
Tell God what you need,
and thank him for all he has done.

Philippians 4:6

Day Fifty-Two

Spiritual Antivenom

*Watch out that no poisonous root of bitterness
grows up to trouble you, corrupting many.*

Hebrew 12:15

At my last annual checkup, I told the doctor I thought I had a spider bite. He told me spiders don't bite. (Clearly, he'd never seen the movie *Spiderman*.)

I'd been working in the yard a few days earlier and bore what I considered evidence, but I listened as Doc observed and explained. After all, he was the one with *MD* behind his name.

Spiders don't bite in the way we think of biting, he said. Rather, they inject venom into their prey, let it do its work, then suck out the liquefied insides.

Eww.

It's the *venom* from a black widow or brown recluse that causes problems, not their teeny tiny bite.

Doc gave me a prescription to treat a mild skin infection, told me I was healthy as a horse, and sent me on my way.

It just so happened that during this time of the physical "spider bite," I was also suffering emotional stings of resentment and self-pity. Pretty noxious attacks, those, and it didn't take an arachnologist to make the metaphorical connection.

If I had been the victim of a black widow, antivenom (antivenin) would have been administered.

As the victim of resentment and self-pity, I knew these initially minor irritations could mutate into bitterness if I left them unchecked. I knew they would poison me on several levels, eventually paralyzing me emotionally and spiritually. And by nature of the toxin, the infection would spread to those around me.

The choice was mine: Cling to these reactions and let them infect me or find an antidote and heal.

In the book of Job we read that resentment kills a fool, and envy slays the simple (Job 5:2). But praise and gratitude are incredibly effective against the venom of resentment and self-pity. Thanking God for His mercy and goodness takes my eyes off of me and my situation and locks my focus on the Lord.

Heavenly Father, help me continuously take up the antidote that destroys the venom of my enemy and fills me with Your healing. Amen.

Therefore by Him let us continually offer
the sacrifice of praise to God, that is,
the fruit of our lips, giving thanks to His name.

Hebrews 13:15 NKJV

Day Fifty-Three

The Garbage Man

*He has removed our sins as far from us
as the east is from the west.*

Psalm 103:12

Tuesday mornings I can hear the garbage truck as it makes the corner down the road from my house. I'm on an every-other-week pickup schedule, and this last "other week" was a doozy. Every time I walked past the big blue roller bin behind the house, I gagged on fear that my local sanitation engineer wouldn't pick it up.

I had put the remains of a roasted chicken in the bin early the first week. You know, those seasoned chickens you get from the market's deli section that cost twice as much as roasting one yourself but smell sooooo good.

By the second week, that chicken carcass did not smell so good.

I watched from the window that Tuesday morning as the garbage man set the roller bin in the electronic arms that lifted it above the truck's cavernous belly and dumped it.

God bless him.

God bless all those men and women for the job they do. Can you imagine what our homes and property would look (and smell) like without those faithful workers? And yes, I know. There was a time when we did not have the luxury or need for sanitation engineers and trash collectors, and if we weren't so wasteful now, etc., etc.

The point is, the garbage man made me think of Jesus.

Before you light a fire at my feet, think about it for a second. Sin stinks. It's rank, and over time it gets worse. We can't take care of our sin ourselves. All the religious perfume and spiritual air fresheners in the world will not cover the odor of sin. It rots. We need it removed.

Jesus does that for us and more. He doesn't just take it away like the garbage man took my chicken carcass. He *paid* for my sin with His *life.* He didn't have any dead rotting sin of His own, but He took mine on Himself and paid my penalty of death.

And when He took it away, He removed it a lot farther than just across the county to the landfill.

It's possible to go to the landfill and see the piles. Be reminded that my trash is in there.

When God removes our sin, He separates it from us as far as the east is from the west. And that's a lot farther than north from south. North and south meet. As you circle the globe from one pole to the other, they meet and turn back on each other, even though you keep moving straight ahead.

East and west never meet.

When God separates me from my sin, I'm not going to run into it someday—unless I deliberately turn around and go back to it. If I keep going straight ahead with Him, I'm not going to stumble into that rotting, decomposing pile of poor choices.

Thank You, God, for Your incredible power to forgive and *cleanse* me from sin. Thank You that I don't have to carry it around on my back, for You have done away with it. Praise You! Amen.

You will cast all our sins into the depths of the sea.

Micah 7:19 NKJV

Day Fifty-Four

A Prequel to Eternity

No eye has seen, no ear has heard,
and no mind has imagined what God
has prepared for those who love him.

1 Corinthians 2:9

I have often heard preachers and teachers describe our temporal existence as a blip on a radar screen compared to unending eternity. I believe they are correct, based on several Scriptures that support their line of thinking, such as Psalm 103:15–16:

> *Our days on earth are like grass;*
> *like wildflowers, we bloom and die.*
> *The wind blows, and we are gone —*
> *as though we had never been here.*

However, while living in this flower of flesh and bone, it is hard to comprehend eternity beyond the "forever" it takes when I wait at the DMV, post office, or supermarket checkout line. I suspect the real forever can't be measured because it is outside of time.

While I recently considered the idea of time-lessness compared to the insta-world in which we live, a thought slipped through my musings:

"This is just the prequel."

Suddenly I understood.

Authors often write prequels to a series after they've written the series. The shorter novellas give the backstory for characters' lives before major events. Prequels allow new readers a quick taste of what's to come in the full-length books they have yet to read.

Two famous book prequels are

The Magician's Nephew and *The Family Corleone,* — written after the original The Chronicles of Narnia and The Godfather series respectively. And there is heated debate over whether *The Hobbit* is the prequel to *The Lord of the Rings*, even though it was written first.

Some memorable movie prequels are

The Good, The Bad, and the Ugly, *Bumblebee*, and a whole slew of *Star Wars* films—all written after the original series.

However, I believe God plans better than the rest of us do. The life we live now is a very abbreviated introduction to grander things to come. And the choices we make now in this brief moment will impact how and where we spend eternity.

Viewing this life as a prequel helped settle some unanswered questions for me. It helped me see the continuity of my story—God's story—and generated even more hope than I had before, based on "the big picture." Because of Jesus and His sacrifice, we have a priceless inheritance "that is kept in heaven for you, pure and undefiled, beyond the reach of change and decay" (1 Peter 1:4).

Life just got a little more exciting, overflowing with promise. If the flowers of the field look as good as they do now, imagine what they look like in eternity.

Oh, God, what an incredible story You have written for us. Thank You for bringing us into life everlasting through Jesus. We love and praise you. Amen.

I go to prepare a place for you.
And if I go and prepare a place for you,
I will come again and receive you to Myself;
that where I am, there you may be also.

John 14:2–3 NKJV

Day Fifty-Five

The River

Jesus stood and said in a loud voice,
"Let anyone who is thirsty come to me and drink.
Whoever believes in me, as Scripture has said,
rivers of living water will flow from within them."

John 7:37–38 NIV

Mountain snowmelt feeds the headwaters of the Arkansas River a couple hundred miles from where I live in Colorado. Roaring against boulders and crashing through canyons, it persists in its course until it slows to a whisper where goslings may paddle in shallows near my home. Regardless of its mood or season, the water is always new. If I wade into the current, it won't be the same water I stepped into the day before, but it will be the same river.

Steady and constant. The same yet different.

A group of praying women I know reminds me of the Arkansas River. Collectively, they have become a current of praise and petition that surges through our community, swirling around boulders of sickness and washing over sun-drenched sandbars of depression. The current carries life wherever its water is needed. I have often felt its pulsing force.

When Jesus spoke of the river of water flowing from the hearts of those who believed in Him, He was speaking of the Holy Spirit (John 7:39). That river never runs dry and rushes full of abundant life.

Much like the Arkansas River that flows out of Colorado's Rocky Mountains, the River of Life from Jesus brings new, fresh water, yet it is always the same river.

One of the mysteries of God.

These are challenging times in which we live. If you don't have a collective river of prayer that you can go to for nourishment and comfort, find one. If you don't have a small group of people who pray, start one. Mingle your river with the rivers of other believers and discover the magnificence of praise and prayer.

There is more life force than we may have realized in the power of corporate prayer. For where two or more gather in His name, He is there in their midst (Matthew 18:20).

Lord, thank You for giving us life through the river of Your Spirit within us. Amen.

The Spirit and the bride say, "Come."
Let anyone who hears this say, "Come."
Let anyone who is thirsty come. Let anyone
who desires drink freely from the water of life."

Revelation 22:17

Day Fifty-Six

A Reminder That God Is There

For You, LORD, have made me glad through Your work;
I will triumph in the works of Your hands.

Psalm 92:4 NKJV

The doorbell rang.

A friendly young man greeted me from a company I had done business with for several years.

After leaving his delivery, he mentioned the deer in my driveway and yard. He had encountered them on the roads in town, a common occurrence, but he hadn't been as close to one as he was out here in the country.

For some reason, my deer gave him pause, and we chatted for several minutes about how beautiful they were.

He turned back down the walkway, and as he got to his van he said, "I needed to see animals today."

His comment was one of the strangest I'd heard.

Why did he need to see animals?

What had his day been like?

Was he battling discouragement? Disappointment? Depression?

Did he live so detached from nature that he had forgotten there is more to life than computerized schedules and delivery routes?

Something about the wildlife touched him and he recognized its effect.

We never know what's going on in the life of someone we meet unexpectedly—what struggles they face, what despair dogs their steps. Do they need a reminder that God is there and He cares about them? Do they need a reminder that God even exists?

Our choice of words, decision to smile, or determination to make eye contact and not be in a hurry could make a big difference.

It doesn't take much to lift someone's spirit.

Let's not overlook any opportunity.

Even if it's merely observing and commenting on one of God's amazing creatures in our yard.

Father, thank You for the wonders of Your creation and for sharing its beauty and grace with us. Help us see Your fingerprints and share the peace of Your blessings with those around us. Amen.

For ever since the world was created,
people have seen the earth and sky. Through everything
God made, they can clearly see his invisible qualities —
his eternal power and divine nature.
So they have no excuse for not knowing God.

Romans 1:20

Day Fifty-Seven

The Cat Who Came in from the Cold . . . for a While

There is more than enough room in my Father's home.

John 14:2

Imagine my surprise when I walked into my attached garage one morning and found the shredded remains of the mini blinds hanging from the single window.

I didn't know feral cats could do such damage, but I learned. They resent having their exit blocked on an eat-and-run visit.

"Annie" was a pretty little tortie (tortoise-shell markings) who showed up one summer with three kittens. We trapped the four of them, changed mama's mind about having more babies in the future, and found homes for the friendly not-yet-feral kitties.

When Annie returned, she'd show up in the morning and evening for breakfast and dinner, but the rest of the time she was very independent.

I couldn't get close to her, much less touch her. But she "talked" to me and liked hanging around when I was outside.

At first, I fed her out by the blue spruce where she hid from the heat. Over the months, I moved the food dish closer to the garage, and eventually inside the garage and up onto the top of the dryer.

Next, I started working with her on the cat door (the raccoons figured it out on their own), and she began to come and go as she pleased. Until I blocked her exit one night.

She took her frustration out on the mini blinds, didn't eat a bite, and sat up by the window "yelling" at me every time I entered the garage.

I had hoped she would see what great accommodations I offered: unlimited food and water, warmth when it's cold or snowy, and two soft beds from which to choose, both up high with unobstructed views.

But when I blocked her in, she refused to eat a morsel and sat up by the window yowling.

The nerve.

I let her out.

Coyotes lurk in the area. Subzero temperatures make for brittle winter nights. Rain and wind are wet and tiring. Always hiding gets old. I'd hoped she'd realize what a great thing it would be to become my cat. The garage and its easy access could be cat heaven, right?

Wrong.

I did everything I could to convince her of my affection other than become a cat myself. How else could I explain that I liked her and wanted her to have a better life?

But it was her choice.

Some people—er, cats—just don't get it, do they?

Thank You, Father, for giving us free will and the freedom to choose You. Thank You for not forcing us, but please, help us not be stubborn and short-sighted when it comes to Your love. Amen.

I am the door.
If anyone enters by Me, he will be saved,
and will go in and out and find pasture.

John 10:9 NKJV

Day Fifty-Eight

Getting from Here to There

Behold, I make all things new.

Revelation 21:5 NKJV

Transition is not one of my favorite words. It implies hard work, change, letting go of the familiar, and heading into the unknown. It takes a person from what was to what will be and often involves pain. Biological mothers everywhere know exactly what I'm talking about.

So do daddies watching daughters glide down the aisle in white dresses, and employees leaving the nest of comfort on the wings of promotion.

As a novelist, I face transition in nearly every scene I write. How does Fernando get from his Ford and into his front room? How does Paula get from dinners for one to picnics in the park for two? Transition.

And how do winter cookie-eaters get from their sweatpants into summer swimsuits? They call a personal trainer.

My son worked as a personal trainer for several years. He helped people change. He taught them how to go from pudgy to perfect, and he even used special exercises called—you guessed it—transitional exercises.

For example, if a client was working muscle set A, and wanted to move to muscle set B, my son took them from an exercise for set A, into an exercise that used both set A and B, and then into one that used only set B. Sounds logical, but it's hard work.

Transition is everywhere. We can't get away from it, and we shouldn't want to. The push from here to there keeps us moving forward. It squeezes life from boney winter branches into new spring buds and strengthens the flabby muscles of sedentary dessert lovers.

Spiritual transition isn't easy either, but we have Someone who promised to get us through it—a very Personal Trainer. As we take those first steps toward peace and balance, we can look to the God who knows what's coming and trust Him to take care of us along the way.

It's never too late for new.

Thank You, Lord, for Your willingness to help us up out of our slumps and self-indulgences, and for getting us on the path to strength and health in You. Amen.

Don't be afraid, for I am with you.
Don't be discouraged, for I am your God.
I will strengthen you and help you.
I will hold you up with my victorious right hand.

Isaiah 41:10

Day Fifty-Nine

Words Are a Big Deal

And a small rudder makes a huge ship turn
wherever the pilot chooses to go,
even though the winds are strong.

James 3:4

I spend a lot of time looking at words and how similar one can be to another, such as *rapid* and *rabid*. One letter can make all the difference.

Do the characters in my novels whimper or whisper?

Do they pick up a glove or a globe?

Am I uniformed or uninformed? Do I inhibit or inhabit?

Words are wiggly little things. The arrangement of letters can create quite a stir if we get them wrong: compliant, complaint. Untied or united.

We may cringe at the middle school reminder of the "parts of speech," but if we use a word as a verb (action word), it might also work as a noun (thing) in a different setting:

Time flies like an arrow; fruit flies like a banana.

And those little marks between the letters also have the ability to change the meaning of a sentence:

What do I have left to write?
What do I have, left to right?
Woman without her man is nothing.
Woman: without her, man is nothing.

So often, it is the small, seemingly insignificant things that make huge differences in our world. How would someone lift food to his mouth without an elbow? How would someone run a race without a knee? Keep their balance without toes?

Do you ever feel that you are small and insignificant in God's view? Do you see yourself as unimportant in the grand scheme of life?

You may feel inconsequential, but you're not. You make more of a difference than you think. Never underestimate the call of God on your life. He has a purpose for each and every one of us.

Get close enough to Him to find out what that purpose is. Be quiet enough to hear His voice. He will tell you.

And remember, it's a very small mark on the paper that makes the great difference between a lie and a life.

Thank You, Father, that no one is insignificant in Your eyes. Thank You that Your eye is not only on the sparrow but on me as well. Amen.

The kingdom of heaven is like a mustard seed,
which a man took and planted in his field.
Though it is the smallest of all seeds, yet when it grows,
it is the largest of garden plants and becomes a tree,
so that the birds come and perch in its branches.

Matthew 13:31–32 NIV

Day Sixty

A Sense of Place

You are my hiding place;
You shall preserve me from trouble;
You shall surround me with songs of deliverance.

Psalm 32:7 NKJV

Have you ever felt as if a comment, a piece of artwork, or something else was out of place because it just didn't fit?

Have you ever felt out of place yourself, as if you didn't belong?

For people, a sense of belonging is critical, and that's why community is so important. People need to feel they have a place to go and others to whom they can turn with common ideals and beliefs.

My church is such a place for me. I feel accepted, whether I am happy and talkative or subdued and quiet. In truth, the church itself is not the building but the people gathered in it. Sometimes we meet in a local park, and even there we are still a church, a body of believers.

Stress sends some people looking for an escape to their "happy place"—usually a peaceful mountain scene, a beach, or a country setting where they "go" in their thoughts.

Those who grieve visit a cemetery, stopping at the grave of a loved one for a thoughtful moment. Others return to the site where ashes were spread, knowing full well that the person is not there. Only their "earth suit" remains.

Regardless, a specific place often helps us feel connected to a loved one.

God has always known how important a sense of place is to us, and in His Word we find several references to it:

Take your sandals off your feet,
for the place where you stand is holy ground

(Exodus 3:5 NKJV)

He who dwells in the secret place of the Most High
shall abide under the shadow of the Almighty

(Psalm 91:1 NKJV)

I go to prepare a place for you. And if I go and
prepare a place for you,

I will come again and receive you to Myself;
that where I am, there you may be also.

(John 14:2–3 NKJV)

For most of my life, I have not consciously considered the importance of place, other than the seventeenth-century mantra for orderliness: "A place for everything and everything in its place."

But now, the truism applies to much more than I once thought, and I find great comfort in knowing I have one.

God knows how we value a sense of place. He planted that need within us so He could give us the perfect location. And He has one for you if you ask Him.

Thank You, Lord, for knowing our needs before we even realize them ourselves. Thank You for providing all of those needs for us in Your perfect timing and grace. Amen.

And the LORD said, "Here is a place by Me,
and you shall stand on the rock."

Exodus 33:21 NKJV

Day Sixty-One

Sidetracked

Don't get sidetracked;
keep your feet from following evil.

Proverbs 4:27

Life speaks to us metaphorically all the time. Consider the word *sidetracked*. It dates back to the old railroad days of the 1870s when a railway siding allowed train cars to move off the main track and onto a side track.

Figuratively speaking, to be sidetracked is to be diverted from the original purpose.

I know for a fact that it's easy to get sidetracked. No engineers or switches required.

The Bible tells us to carefully choose the path we take in life, make sure it is the Lord's path, and stick to it. Sadly, my attention and curiosity have often wandered, diverting me from the main path to interesting-looking frontage roads. And sometimes I've focused on the horizon when what I needed to watch for was right in front of me.

My pastor says if we are looking for direction about some place to serve, we should do what is "right here." Then he waves his hand in front of his face. That's a good way of putting it.

God doesn't hide His will for us in a deep dark cave and wait for us to find it. I believe He makes it clear—if we're paying attention.

One of my life verses is Psalm 16:11 (NIV): "You make known to me the path of life." I can say that is absolutely the case. God has shown me, through His Word, the pathway to life.

I love the wording of Proverbs 4:25–27 in the New Living Translation:

> *Look straight ahead, and fix your eyes*
> *on what lies before you.*
> *Mark out a straight path for your feet;*
> *stay on the safe path.*
> *Don't get sidetracked;*
> *keep your feet from following evil.*

So why is it that I have often left the safe path and let side tracks and frontage roads draw me away?

Because I am fallible. But God is not, and He constantly steers me back on course when I look to Him for help. Our human nature wants things its own way, and without seeking the Lord's guidance, I'm likely to make as good a choice as Adam and Eve did in the garden of Eden—even though they knew better.

In spite of the human condition, I find hope in Psalm 25:4–5:

> *Show me the right path, O LORD;*
> *Point out the road for me to follow.*
> *Lead me by your truth and teach me,*
> *For you are the God who saves me.*
> *All day long I put my hope in you.*

I typed this verse out and taped copies in key places around the house. Like the bathroom mirror. The refrigerator door. My closet. It's a great encouragement.

If you have a favorite verse that speaks to your heart, print it out and tape it up in places you'll see it and be reminded to stay on the main track.

Life is full of diversions. We need all the reminders we can get.

Thank You, Lord, for Your faithfulness to encourage me again and again, showing me which path to take. Help me be patient enough to wait and listen for Your direction. Amen.

All day long I put my hope in you.

Psalm 25:5

Day Sixty-Two

Deep unto Deep

From the depths of despair, O LORD,
I call for your help.

Psalm 130:1

Most of us have seen iconic images of Niagara Falls frozen in time—a massive, hanging wall of immovable ice. The first time I saw the wintry phenomenon I was stunned, thinking my eyes betrayed me or the image had been photo-shopped. How could such thunderous, rushing water be stopped in its journey?

I've never been to New York or the Niagara River, and I hope someday to make the trip. But I have heard the roar of the mighty Shoshone Falls on the Snake River near Twin Falls, Idaho. I've seen the rapids of Great Falls, Montana, and understood the eighteen-mile portage of canoes by Lewis, Clark, and their companions along that stretch of the Missouri River in 1805.

And I love the pivotal scene in *The Last of the Mohicans* partially filmed behind the cascading Bridal Veil Falls in North Carolina.

How humbling to stand near such a display of natural strength.

These locations bring to mind one of my favorite Scriptures which speaks of "the noise of Your waterfalls" (Psalm 42:7 NKJV). But it is what precedes that phrase that captures more than my attention: "Deep calls unto deep."

What does that even mean?

As I searched for a definition, I read several versions of this Scripture and settled upon the poetry of The Passion Translation as the psalmist cries out to God:

> *My deep need calls out to the*
> *deep kindness of your love.*

That rings true in the recesses of my own heart. No one knows me quite so well as God, not even my family. The deep longing of my soul is equaled only to the deep love of the Creator.

People who suffer similar grief will often share similar grace with each other. They recognize the deep wounds of another person as well as the need for a deep dependency upon God.

If you have found someone like that, treasure them. If you have not discovered that the depth of God's love will meet the depth of your need, talk to Him. Pour out your pain. Be honest in your complaint, for He knows anyway.

And take heart in the next verse of Psalm 42, the one that assures us of God's response:

Thank You, Lord, for knowing the depths of my pains and worries and fears. Thank You that none of them are out of Your reach. Please, show me Your great compassion and care. Amen.

The LORD will command His lovingkindness
in the daytime,
And in the night His song shall be with me —
A prayer to the God of my life.

Psalm 42:8 NKJV

Day Sixty-Three

Thirsty

Please, give me a drink.
John 4:7

Do you ever get so busy that you ignore other people? So tied up in your own thoughts that you miss the obvious? In too big of a hurry to sense their need? I do.

Maybe that's why I enjoy reading how Jesus met people one-on-one and always had something pertinent to say to them. The way He noticed them.

One example of this is the hot, dry day He stopped to rest on his trip north from Judea. He stopped at the well of Sychar in Samaria, which was unusual, because most Jews went out of their way to skirt around Samaria.

Except Jesus.

When a woman showed up to draw water from the well, Jesus asked her for a drink. Seems logical, but it wasn't. Women didn't go to the public well in the middle of the day. They went in the morning with other women so they could catch up on news and family events.

And men in that society didn't speak to women in public, especially Jewish men to Samaritan women.

Except Jesus.

That day, the woman may have thought a stranger in the area—a Jew no less—would simply ignore her.

But Jesus knew exactly why she came to the well in the middle of the day, and He offered her what she was really looking for.

He wasn't in too big of a hurry to talk with her. He didn't brush her off.

He wasn't like me in the checkout line at the market, avoiding the eyes of others because I'm in a hurry or bothered about something that needs my uninterrupted thought processes.

He wasn't at all like me squeezing into an airline seat and staring out the window hoping no one talked to me so I could zone out during the flight.

Nor was He like me in the post office wearing sunglasses because I have a lot on my mind. Easy in, easy out. No chit-chat.

No, He wasn't like me at all. He spoke to her, told her He knew she was living with man number six, but showed no offense or judgement. He used a metaphor at hand to teach an eternal truth about living water—better than what the well offered—and where to find it.

But He is also telling me something here. He's showing me how to meet people where they live. In the middle of their need. Maybe in my checkout line at the market, or the seat next to me on a plane.

Jesus didn't always follow the standards of society. Imagine that.

So now the choice is mine. In the weeks ahead, will I make the most of what could be God-ordained opportunities to show a little interest in someone else's life? Or will I draw into myself, ignore the situation, and let the other person go away thirsty?

Thank You, Lord, for reminding me how important individuals are to You. Help me see through Your eyes the "extra" people in my daily life and reach out to them. Amen.

Those who drink the water I give
will never be thirsty again.

John 4:14

Day Sixty-Four

Don't Listen to the Doubt

Let us make human beings in our image, to be like us.
Genesis 1:26

Have you ever suffered from "imposter syndrome"? Misgivings about what you've been called to do.

"Me—teach?"

"Me—sing?"

"Me—help the sick/poor/lonely?"

As an author, I know well the spidery footsteps of doubt that crawl up my shoulder as I sit at my computer . . . "Me—write?"

Oh, it gets even better: "Making up stories is a worthless occupation. What good can fiction possibly do? And romantic fiction? Ha! What a joke."

And then I walk into a restaurant, an airport, or even my doctor's office and see artwork and photographs that tell the story of my preferred genre—the West.

Colorful cowboys, running horses, log cabins huddled near mountain streams. Old barns and corrals stretching out before extravagant sunsets. I want to climb into those pictures and escape for a while. Smell dawn sifting through a forest, hear the nicker of a horse at feed time. Run my fingers through the scruff of a good cow dog.

Someone took those photographs or painted those pictures, someone with a creative gift that touches my heart and offers me the respite I need.

That's when I understand why readers thank me for the escape they find in my stories.

You who teach and open the eyes of understanding, you who prepare a meal for someone who needs it or give an hour or a day to those who are sick, hurting, or lonely—you are helping to restore souls. You are offering an escape from the suffering, if only for a moment.

Don't listen to the doubt that tries to strip away your God-given gift.

You are offering respite.

There is restorative value in the gift of giving, whether food, time, physical help, or a listening ear. There is restorative value in song, story, art, and countless other creative expressions.

Thank God He poured creativity into His children. Thank God that He lets us walk in His image and share in His touch.

How gracious He is.

Thank You, Creator God, for imprinting Yourself upon me and blessing me with gifts chosen specifically for me. Help me recognize and use them for Your glory. Amen.

Whether you turn to the right or to the left, your ears will hear a voice behind you, saying, "This is the way; walk in it."

Isaiah 30:21 NIV

Day Sixty-Five

Satan Is a Liar
Part 1 of 2

Be sober, be vigilant; because your adversary
the devil walks about like a roaring lion,
seeking whom he may devour.

1 Peter 5:8 NKJV

Whom he may devour. Sounds gruesome, doesn't it? Like something out of a zombie movie. However, there is more devouring going on than we realize.

A friend of mine had her computer hacked the other day, and the culprit obtained access to her bank account. Thankfully, the bank stopped the bleeding before it was too late, and all of my friend's funds were recovered.

When my credit card was compromised last year, I had to cancel it, stop payment, and get a new card. Thankfully, the company worked with me when I discovered the bogus purchases and didn't charge me for them. (This is why I match receipts with every purchase every month to combat theft.)

Lately, I've received countless attempts via text messaging, phone calls, email, and social media to bait me into clicking on a link. If I'm not careful, a fake threat or prize gimmick can lure me into trouble. If I'm not ever-vigilant, an imposter can worm their way into my online accounts and personal information. So I must beware!

This is not new advice.

A couple thousand years ago, a fisherman named Peter said, "Beware, because your enemy, Satan, is out looking for a victim" (1Peter 5:8, my paraphrase).

Various translations of the Bible state the warning in different ways:

Be alert and of sober mind.
Stay alert! Watch out.
Be sober-minded; watch.
Be vigilant.
Be on the alert.
Be clear-minded and alert.
Be self-controlled.
Discipline yourselves, keep alert.

Alert seems to be the word of choice. When it comes to daily communication, I am not always as alert as I should be when I scroll through text messages and email. That can make me a target.

The same applies to my spiritual life. I want to stay in the truth of God's Word and know it well enough that I'm not tricked by a twist of terms, as Eve was deceived by the serpent's misquote in Eden.

Lord, be my light and truth, and help me stay alert not only to the deception around me but to the strength of Your Word. Be my shield. Thank You. Amen.

But You, O Lord, are a shield around me.

Psalm 3:3 NIV

Day Sixty-Six

Satan Is a Liar
Part 2 of 2

He was a murderer from the beginning.
He has always hated the truth,
because there is no truth in him.
When he lies, it is consistent with his character;
for he is a liar and the father of lies.

John 8:44

Jesus said He is the way, the truth, and the life (John 14:6). He also told us that Satan is a liar. Seems simple, right? It is, but the liar never comes right out and tells us that he is lying.

The technological dangers of our world today can mirror situations from our spiritual and physical lives. For example:

- Temptation comes when we least expect it.
- The test is always a pop quiz—we have to be ready.

- If we're not watching, we'll step in the hole.
- No matter how it's said, it pays to pay attention.

So how do we know if something or someone is on the level or pulling a fast one? How do we determine real information from fake, truth from lies?

- If we know the rules of engagement when it comes to email and social media, we'll be less likely to fall for a scam.
- If we're familiar with our list of friends on social media, we'll know something is up when they ask to be our "friend" again.

With the increase of online trolling, I'm beginning to see the urgency in Peter's words for both my spiritual life and my technological life as well. Today's hackers are a great metaphor for Satan's tactics. In the same way that Satan looks for someone to devour, hackers troll the internet, looking for someone to attack and consume—someone who isn't aware of scams and trickery, someone who is susceptible to deceit.

So take the fisherman's advice and beware!

The Message puts it this way: "Keep a cool head. Stay alert. The Devil is poised to pounce and would like nothing better than to catch you napping. Keep your guard up" (1 Peter 5:8–9).

The first time I saw this scriptural warning, I wondered why Satan would go to such lengths to trip me up. I have learned since then that he wants to disable me. He comes only to steal, kill, and destroy, just like Jesus said.

Jesus's purpose is to give us a rich and satisfying life (see John 10:10). If we familiarize ourselves with God's Word, we'll recognize a convenient twist away from the truth.

Help us, Lord, to be so familiar with Your Word that we recognize a scam. Socially, help us be diligent stewards of Your gifts and act wisely in this world. Thank You. Amen.

Test all things; hold fast what is good.
1 Thessalonians 5:21

Day Sixty-Seven

Time

*A thousand years in your sight are like a day
that has just gone by, or like a watch in the night.*

Psalm 90:4 NIV

Time.

We run out of it faster than we run out of money and milk.

However, we can always get more money and milk. We can't buy more time.

When I was growing up and my mother didn't want to accept an invitation, she always said, "We're too busy. We don't have time." It was a common mantra, bless her, but I never understood what we were so busy doing.

A couple of years ago, I took one of my books to a woman I'd met in a local nursing home after she mentioned she'd like to read it. Weeks later when I saw her again, she said, "I haven't read your book yet. I haven't had the time."

I thought of Mother. What else was this wheel-chair-bound woman doing? Time was something there seemed to be a lot of in the nursing home. Was busyness just an excuse? Or did this dear lady have difficulty holding the book or seeing clearly? Could she no longer read?

Maybe she just wanted to *have* it since she had no visitors.

I wish now I had taken the *time* to read it to her.

Someday, rather than running out of the little blocks into which we chop time like minutes, hours, and years, we will lose it altogether. There will *be* no time. Not in the sense of "time's up," or "you're past the time limit," but in the sense that time will no longer exist.

It will be over.

Done.

Not a thing.

This realization was a bit chilling for me. I thought of family members who have not chosen to follow Jesus. Someday, they will not have that choice because time will be gone.

When God gave us free choice, He gave us time in which to exercise it. When time as we know it ceases to be, so will our ability to choose where we want to spend Forever. The phrase *too late* will become a bottomless reality. Hence the importance of choosing Jesus now. "Today is the day of salvation" (2 Corinthians 6:2).

God exists in timelessness and is not limited as we are by time and space.

Death is the great fear that haunts time-trapped people, yet Jesus beat it. He crushed it for us because we couldn't. Don't let time run out on you. If you haven't chosen Him, please do so while time is still a thing.

Thank You, God, for allowing us to choose You. Thank You for doing what we could not. Give us the opportunity and boldness to share this good news with our family and friends. Amen.

The Lord is not slow in keeping his promise,
as some understand slowness. Instead he is
patient with you, not wanting anyone to perish,
but everyone to come to repentance.

2 Peter 3:8–9 NIV

Day Sixty-Eight

Out of the Stump

Out of the stump of David's family will grow a shoot —
yes, a new Branch bearing fruit from the old root.

Isaiah 11:1

Last summer, a tree in our young orchard was accidentally snapped off about six inches above ground level. Distressing, to say the least, and costly as well. It had to be replaced.

My husband dug up the stump and tossed it aside to make room for a new tree. A couple of weeks later, instead of throwing it away, he put the stump and its root ball in a bucket and added water to see what would happen.

The dried-out stump just sat there in the bucket looking mutilated, forlorn, and forgotten. But as they say, appearances can be deceiving.

Several days later, it sprouted.

The resurrected stump reminded me of how often I mistakenly think defeat is the end. That failure is final and everything is too late.

This may be true in certain cases, such as a missed field goal attempt that would have put one football team ahead of the other before the game's end.

But I believe in most situations, this sentiment is not true. And more often than that, I believe it is one of our enemy's greatest weapons.

Satan may not succeed in tempting us away from godly living, but he's very good at disabling us with doubt and discouragement. We shut down and become depressed and ineffective.

So how do we counter the attack?

By getting ourselves in the right place with the necessary nutrients. We need the spiritual counterparts of what the tree stump needed: soil, water, and light, and God has them all in abundant supply.

When we spend time with followers of Christ and get into God's Word, we start healing and growing.

The Bible tells us to let our roots go down deep into the soil of God's marvelous love (Ephesians 3:17). Jesus said He is the Light of the world (John 8:12) and that those who believe in Him will have rivers of living water flowing from within them (John 7:38).

No, failure is not final—unless we're talking about eternity and failure to trust Jesus. How many chances do we get to choose Him before we die? If we keep waiting and we hit eternity without Him, it *will* be too late. Failure to take God at His word is final and fatal.

But choosing Him now is life renewed.

Thank You, Father, for the second chances You give us—for renewal and refreshment and the opportunity to sprout anew for You. Amen.

For there is hope for a tree, if it is cut down,
that it will sprout again,
and that its tender shoots will not cease.

Job 14:7 NKJV

Day Sixty-Nine

The Rest of the Story

The first to speak in court sounds right—
until the cross-examination begins.

Proverbs 18:17

As an author who lacks sketching and painting skills, I often sidestep artsy remarks by confessing that the only thing I can draw is a conclusion.

Joking aside, I believe this holds true for many of us. We are often quick to judge before we have all the facts. We decide yea or nay when we have only a sliver of the picture.

A perfect illustration presented itself one morning as my husband and I drove across Kentucky on the way to a friend's house. Traveling a four-lane state highway through rolling green hills, we came upon a city policeman walking along the shoulder toward the city we'd just left. A little farther on, we passed his parked cruiser.

A half-mile later came a woman walking on the shoulder headed the same direction as the officer.

And not too far past her, we found her car parked on the edge of the road.

Was the woman walking toward the police car hoping to find help? Did she run out of gas, patience, or time? Had the officer been tailing her—perhaps his estranged girlfriend or wife—and changed his mind? Had they just had a fight? Was she walking back to apologize?

Had the radio gone out in the officer's cruiser, requiring him to hike back to headquarters? Didn't he have a phone? Why weren't either of them driving? Were both vehicles sabotaged by a bank-heist suspect or a ten-year-old kid on a joy ride? Okay, maybe not.

We'll never know what was going on that day or if those people even knew each other.

It's quite similar to situations I find myself in, such as a restaurant where the service is slow (because other waitstaff called off and the young, single-mother, college-student is doing her best to keep up). Or when I get stuck behind an elderly man in slow motion at the grocery store checkout (because he can't see his credit cards through tears since the recent death of his wife who did all the shopping).

We cross paths with people like this every day, and we know nothing about them. Sadly, we often act like we're the only person who is busy, hurried, stressed, late, or angry because things aren't going our way.

We don't know their whole story. We don't see the full picture.

Jesus knew the heart of man and He told us to go the extra mile . . . love our neighbor . . . pray for our enemies . . . forgive and be forgiven . . . treat others the way we want to be treated.

These are challenging commands. But the more we familiarize ourselves with *His* story, the more strength we'll find to be . . . different.

We don't always get to know the rest of the story. But we get to know the story of the One who saves the rest of us if we let Him.

Thank You, Lord, for caring. Help us do the same. Amen.

But a Samaritan, as he traveled,
came where the man was;
and when he saw him, he took pity on him.

Luke 10:33 NIV

Day Seventy

Circle of Service

There are different kinds of service,
but we serve the same Lord.
God works in different ways,
but it is the same God who does the work in all of us.

Romans 12:5–6

I prefer to shop for groceries early in the morning. That doesn't mean I always make it, I just prefer it. There are fewer people and more shopping carts. Shelves are recently stocked, and the nerves of checkers and staff are not yet filed down to the nubbins.

One morning as I stood in line for the "fast" lane, I gave more than cursory notice of the woman at the self-checkout bank of machines.

She hovered there to help do-it-yourselfers like me who often don't do it the way the machine thinks you should. I learned that she had worked twenty-two years for that store since she first landed the job as an eighteen-year-old high school graduate.

I saw her in a different light that day. She, and others like her, faithfully served the community. Her job mattered to me. It mattered to a lot of people.

And then I realized that my job does too. It's my job to give people something to relax with when they come home in the evening from a hard day on their feet.

It's my job to write an entertaining but encouraging story into which they can escape for a while and then return to their world uplifted. It's my job to write a good book they will enjoy.

Observing readers in their real world helps me realize I could be a blessing to them doing my job as they are a blessing to me doing theirs.

It is a circle of service, one to another.

We all fit somewhere in that circle. Your job matters whether you are working in the market, teaching school, or caring for the aged and ill.

Even retirement is a job. Where are you helping and what are you doing that you didn't have time for before? Who are you listening to over coffee or praying for?

If you're not sure where you fit in the circle of service, ask God to show you. He will.

And remember, some of us are called to be elbows, praise God. How would people eat otherwise?

Thank You, God, that every position in Your kingdom is important. Help me do my best in the place You have called me to serve. Amen.

Each of you should use whatever gift
you have received to serve others,
as faithful stewards of God's grace in its various forms.

1 Peter 4:10 NIV

Day Seventy-One

Wait Is a Verb

Wait on the LORD; be of good courage,
and He shall strengthen your heart;
wait, I say, on the LORD!

Psalm 27:14 NKJV

"No waiting on checkout lane number three."

I squeezed the red plastic handle of my shopping cart and held my ground. The frenzy around me rivaled Indy 500 drivers at the green flag. Shoppers rushed to be first in the new line so they wouldn't have to . . . wait.

What is it about waiting that makes us so antsy?

Several years ago, I worked as a secretary for an agricultural chemical company in northern Colorado. One morning a sales representative came into the office with his golden retriever. The man picked through the donut selection next to the coffee pot and laid one of the smooth, glazed pastries on the floor in front of his dog.

The retriever just sat there staring at the donut. Saliva dripped from its clinched jaws.

"Why won't he eat it?" I asked.

"Because I haven't told him to," the salesman said.

To emphasize his point, he walked away and visited with fellow employees while the retriever stared and drooled. At last, the salesman returned and quietly said, "Okay."

The dog inhaled the donut.

The salesman had trained his dog to eat only at his command. That way, he said, the dog could never be poisoned.

I think God does this with me. He tells me to wait and I start drooling.

Does God want me to stand quietly in line while the bag boy runs to get the can of green beans forgotten by the customer in front of me? Is there a character-building lesson going on?

Is there a reason for sitting with my foot on the brake at a forever traffic light?

Does God's "wait" have a hidden motive behind it? Does it suppress a me-first mentality or jump-start patience?

The word *wait* is an intransitive verb—an action word that does not require an object in the sentence. It can serve as a command.

Psalm 37:7 (NKJV) directs us to "rest in the LORD, and *wait* patiently for Him." This kind of wait encourages me to actively trust that God has a better grasp of the situation than I. It reminds me of the well-trained retriever.

I'm still progressing through the stages of Christian maturity and drooling over what I want. But I know the Lord has greater things for me than a glazed donut. His timing is better than mine, and His command to wait has protected me from making many poor—and dangerous—choices.

Thank You, God, for having my best interest at heart. Help me listen. Amen.

But those who wait on the LORD Shall
renew their strength;

Isaiah 40:31 NKJV

Day Seventy-Two

What's the Question Again?

"Where were you when I laid the earth's foundation?
Tell me, if you understand."

Job 38:4 NIV

If God asked you a question, what would it be?

"God doesn't need to ask me a question," you say. "He already knows everything about me."

True, He does, but God is relational. He has always asked questions of those He loves. Here are a few examples:

- He asked Adam in the Garden of Eden, "Where are you?" (see Genesis 3:9)
- He asked Elijah on Mount Horeb, "Why are you here?" (see 1Kings 19:9,13)
- He asked a blind man, "What do you want me to do for you?" (see Mark 10:51)

The answers all seem pretty obvious, particularly the last one, but I believe God still asks those same questions today.

- Where are you? Is God waiting for you in the cool of the evening or the quiet pre-dawn to talk with you, listen to your concerns, warm you with His presence as you worship Him? Have you missed that appointment often enough that God is whispering, "Where are you?"

- What are you doing here? Have you run away from something the Lord called you to do? Have you thrown up your hands in disgust or discouragement and quit? Are you in the wrong place at the wrong time, wondering how you ended up in a cave and how you got off track?

- What do you want me to do for you? Jesus said we miss out on a lot because we don't ask. What is it *exactly* that you need from Him? Can you pinpoint it? Are you willing to ask, or are you afraid He won't come through with an answer?

An all-knowing God who asks us questions is a personal God who cares about relationship.

What is He asking you?

Oh, Lord, help me pay attention to the questions You whisper to my heart. Amen.

"Why did you doubt me?"

Matthew 14:31

Day Seventy-Three

Rest Is Underrated

He makes me lie down in green pastures.

Psalm 23:2 NIV

My husband and I recently took a few days off and visited family in Washington State.

We worked frantically to get things accomplished ahead of time, making up for the days we would be away. And when we returned home, we worked a little extra to get caught up after being gone.

We felt like we had to work hard to rest.

That sounds ridiculous, I know, but it seems to be what our world has come to. So I'm raising my hand to complain, disagree, and say no.

A couple of years ago, I took a few days off and went to a mountain retreat where I planned to write thousands and thousands of words on my next novel.

No phone (when I turned it off). No chores or cooking or other life distractions. Just writing. Plain and simple work. Work. WORK.

Instead, I rested.

Did I berate myself?

A little. Between naps.

Did I fail?

No.

Did I learn anything important?

Yes.

Rest is underrated.

Rest is necessary.

Rest is a gift.

God did it (see Genesis 2:2–3).

Jesus gives it (see Matthew 11:28–29).

Refreshment follows it (see Psalm 62:1).

We have become so production-oriented that we often miss out on this regenerative blessing.

No matter what you are doing in this season, I pray you will make time for rest. Recharge your batteries. Renew your spirit.

Do what Jesus said:

Come with me by yourselves
to a quiet place and get some rest.

Mark 6:31 NIV

Thank You, Lord, for giving us everything that we need, even rest. Amen.

For he knows how weak we are;
he remembers we are only dust.

Psalm 103:14

Day Seventy-Four

Give Me a Home

The boundary lines have fallen for me
in pleasant places;
surely I have a delightful inheritance.
Psalm 16:6 NIV

Do you know the second line in the classic Western ballad that begins, "Oh, give me a home"? It has something to do with deer, and antelope.

Good job if you remembered. However, the line after that is the best one, in my opinion, and may have been the reason for the song's popularity:

"Where seldom is heard a discouraging word, and the skies are not cloudy all day."[1]

"Home on the Range" became the iconic tune of the American West in the 1800s and was sung by cowboys on the Chisolm Trail and elsewhere. It was popularized in the next century by silver-screen cowboy crooners like Gene Autry.

---

[1] "Home On the Range," Brewster M. Higley, before 1874, Public Domain.

But it's not just the prairie that has changed since Dr. Brewster M. Higley first penned the words in 1873. It's the proliferation of discouraging words.

How many have you heard lately?

Probably more than a few. And I'm not even talking about the news media.

As an author, I hear both positive and negative feedback about my work through public review forums such as Amazon, Goodreads, BookBub, and Facebook. One of my very first reviews years ago was a real slice-and-dicer, yet that book turned out to be a top seller.

"Consider the source," I was told, and there is some comfort in that cliché. But for me, the experience underscored the power of words, both spoken and printed.

Words are like bricks. They can build up or tear down, and it's a whole lot easier to tear down something than to build it. Anyone with a sledgehammer and a crowbar can demolish a house, but it takes a skilled craftsman to construct one.

Our grandparents' generation of school children were taught to deflect painful words with a clever quip: "Sticks and stones may break my bones, but words will never hurt me."

How untrue!

Sticks and stones may break our bones, but words can shred us to ribbons and leave us bleeding in the ditch.

Words have power to heal hearts, but discouraging words can destroy friendships and marriages—like little drops of acid over time, corroding once-loving foundations until nothing is left.

Cruel remarks on social media impact young people more and more every day. Ugly barbs devastate their sense of worth and diminish their character.

May we learn to choose our words wisely and make our homes a refuge where "seldom is heard a discouraging word."

Thank You, Lord, for the power of Your words to comfort and heal us. Amen.

*The very words I have spoken to you
are spirit and life.*

John 6:63

Day Seventy-Five

Dandelion Cowboy

Obviously, I'm not trying to win
the approval of people, but of God.
If pleasing people were my goal,
I would not be Christ's servant.

Galatians 1:10

Most of the characters in my books are people I've cooked up on my own. But some of them sneak up on me when I'm not looking, leaving me with the sense that I've met them before and just can't remember when or where.

Like one of the youngsters in The Cañon City Chronicles series—a little cowboy named Kip. He's the youngest of three brothers, the tag-along. The one who gets left out more often than not.

Recently, I realized where I'd met Kip—though that wasn't his real name. He was a student from my former life as a sixth-grade teacher in rural California, my Dandelion Cowboy.

Each morning he lined up in front of my classroom with the rest of the first-period students. Except he wasn't much like the rest of the students.

In his Wranglers and dusty cowboy boots, he didn't dress like the others. A towhead among dark-haired children, he quietly stuck out in spite of how much he tried not to.

But in the spring when the dandelions sprouted, he was at the front of the line with a short-stemmed bouquet and a shy smile. I'd talk to him about cowboy things and one day commented on the shiny buckle he wore—his trophy for winning an event at a weekend junior rodeo. Most of my other students had no idea what it meant to rope a calf or ride a steer or run a barrel- or pole-pattern on horseback.

The little cowboy was a loner. A throwback perhaps, from a long line of those who preferred the company of their horse and a good view of the herd.

I saw that heritage in the father who came to parent-teacher conferences—a taller, stouter version of my Dandelion Cowboy, in his good palm-leaf hat and square-toed boots.

Creases at his blue eyes cut several shades lighter than the rest of his sunbaked face—the badge of a working man who spent his days in the saddle.

Dad's words were few, but they showed his interest. He wanted his young man to tend to business. Hold up his end of the load. Be a gentleman.

Cowboy morals.

Today when I see a patch of what most people call weeds, I smile and wonder about my Dandelion Cowboy—if he stuck to his ways in spite of the crowd. I hope he's trailing a herd in the California foothills, going to summertime rodeos, and most of all, becoming the fine man I knew he would one day be.

Thank You, Lord, for those who encourage faithfulness in the callings You have given. Help us recognize Your gifts in the children around us and strengthen them in Your ways. Amen.

Train up a child in the way he should go,
and when he is old he will not depart from it.

Proverbs 22:6 NKJV

Day Seventy-Six

Beware the Swinging Chicken

Jesus answered: "Watch out that no one deceives you."
Matthew 24:4 NIV

The farmers' market brimmed with vendors' booths of homemade breads, jellies, candles, and stained glass. Home-grown vegetables covered tables in patches of silk-topped corn, golden peaches, and colorful squash — a fresh-air market spread beneath sunshine and shade, populated by young and old alike. Some came to sell their wares, others to visit or let their children play in the park.

I came to redeem the time.

I had a couple of hours to wait for someone, so I chose the farmers' market as a restful place to sit and read with no interruption, no internet, and no news.

A few minutes into my book, a familiar background noise penetrated my consciousness, and I vaguely wondered why anyone would bring a live chicken to a farmer's market not designated for poultry. Was it a gimmick to draw shoppers to fresh eggs?

Finally, I stopped reading and looked around more closely at my setting.

No chicken.

Hearing the drawn-out cluck again, I turned toward the sound—and there it was. Not a rogue chicken on the loose but a girl on the park swing.

Every time she swung forward, the metal brackets squawked around the old beam like a brooding hen.

I had been certain the sound I heard was a chicken, but clearly it was not. How easily I was fooled.

Just as easily as I'm misled if I'm not paying attention.

Our world today is a noisy place full of modified soundbites, "virtual" images, and artificial intelligence. A lot of people are telling us what truth to believe and who to trust. They insist that their perspective or interpretation is the way things really are. Rarely do they present another side of the issue.

Beware the swinging chicken.

We must look into the facts ourselves, check more than one source, and most importantly, check God's Word. Find out what He says. Learn His ways and follow them.

There's a lot of squawking going on out there. Check it out before you believe it.

Lord, help us not to be deceived by what we think we see and hear, but lead us to Your truths. May we cling to them, for they are the key to life. Amen.

Don't let anyone capture you with empty philosophies and high-sounding nonsense that come from human thinking and from the spiritual powers of this world, rather than from Christ.

Colossians 2:8

Day Seventy-Seven

Come and Drink

Is anyone thirsty? Come and drink.

Isaiah 55:1

Deer munch their way through yards and wood-ed areas in our rural neighborhood. Never hurried and rarely startled, they meander from one home to the next. On early mornings when I walk, I find them drinking at the irrigation pond, and when the water gates open into orchards and pastures, they stand in the cool running streams.

It was in such a stream one afternoon that my husband saw the Loner up close.

The young buck bore a malformed antler that flopped uselessly behind its right ear. Solitary, it foraged but never found enough, for its dull hide clung to ribs that signaled hunger most of the season.

Other imperfections not so easily noticed must have marked it, for it was an outcast from the herd. In the world of nature, these flaws put the fellow at a disadvantage. It didn't attract does during rut and would lose in a battle with another buck. So it stayed to itself rather than run with a bachelor band or graze in the comfort of the family herd.

Yet it still sought water. In spite of its deformities, the need pressed it to skirt irrigated fields, finding respite in shady groves.

I wonder if we are like that solitary deer? Do we pant for the Life-Giver? Do we pursue Him in spite of our imperfections and failures? Our unworthiness. Even if we don't fit in with others, do we seek His presence?

Oh, I pray that we do!

Beneath the wings of our Lord's unending care, we need not fear that He will shun us. He doesn't tell us to go away and come back when we've figured things out or pulled ourselves together. He doesn't say we're not quite ready.

He tells us what we need so desperately to hear …

"If you are thirsty, come. Drink freely from my unlimited source and find life." (Revelation 21:6, my paraphrase).

There is no other source of sustenance than our Creator God.

Let's be like the deer.

Oh, Father, I praise You for Your provision. Thank You for Your tender care of Your creatures and for me as well. You deserve all the glory. Amen.

As the deer pants for streams of water,
so my soul pants for you, my God.

Psalm 42:1 NIV

Day Seventy-Eight

Who Needs Boundaries?

The LORD tears down the house of the proud,
but he sets the widow's boundary stones in place.

Proverbs 15:25 NIV

Skyline Drive winds up the side and along the top of the hogbacks west of Cañon City, Colorado. A favorite of tourists and locals alike, the narrow road lives up to its name, allowing motorists and hikers to feel as if they are scaling the sky.

And there is no railing anywhere along the three-mile stretch.

Some of us don't like that unfettered feeling.

Personally, I appreciate boundaries, especially along bridges and roadways.

Imagine the sea with no sandy hem around its edges. Tsunamis demonstrate what happens when waves overstep their boundary.

Borders are also aesthetically pleasing to the eye. They provide not only protection but beauty and a sense of order. Consider flower gardens, farmland, and lawns. Without boundaries, over-growth and chaos would distract from the land's beauty and productivity.

The Bible has a lot to say about physical boundaries, but it also speaks to our emotional borders, limits that help protect our time, energy, and concentration. Too often we overlook such boundaries, especially when we have trouble saying no to demands on our time and resources.

Boundaries in our daily lives are meant to help us, yet we often ignore them when we eat too much, drink too much, or refuse to follow God's plan for relationships.

Jesus told His followers the story of ten brides-maids awaiting the day of a wedding. Five were foolish and unprepared and five were wise. When the unprepared women asked the others to share their lamp oil for the night, the other five said no. At first, their answer seems selfish and "unchristian." But good stewardship calls for refusal to recklessly give away what we've been charged with. This includes time, resources, and emotional energy.

Bound edges of dishcloths and bath towels keep them from fraying and unraveling. Yet how often do we feel frayed around the edges? Is it because we have no boundaries or limits?

How comforting the words of Psalm 139:5 (NIV) when it says God hems us in "behind and before, and you lay your hand upon me." If we heed the Lord's loving care, He leads us away from regret, overextension, and stress.

Skyline Drive may be an exciting excursion, but when it comes to everyday life and challenges, I thank God for the safeguards He provides.

Thank you, Father, for giving us boundaries and limits. Help us pay attention to the protections You have put in place and for the order You desire for our lives. Amen.

I made the sand a boundary for the sea,
an everlasting barrier it cannot cross.
The waves may roll, but they cannot prevail;
they may roar, but they cannot cross it.

Jeremiah 5:22

Day Seventy-Nine

Of Roots and Fruits

*Let the land sprout with vegetation — every sort
of seed-bearing plant, and trees that grow seed-bearing
fruit. These seeds will then produce the kinds
of plants and trees from which they came.*

Genesis 1:11

Last fall, a cheeky tree squirrel ate the autumn decorations off my front porch. One evening I had two pumpkins and a clutch of Indian corn; the next morning I had one ear of corn with several kernels missing and two hardened pumpkin stems. So much for seasonal décor.

In May, I noticed a strange plant pushing up among the roses in front of our house. By the time the squash-like plant had overtaken the rose garden, green basketballs had formed on several stems, reminding me of the previous autumn's décor debacle.

From the fruit I knew the root.

In the natural world, the connection is easily recognized. The same principle is true in our hearts, but we overlook the spiritual application.

I'm currently reading three books, and last week all three intersected with the root-fruit concept. When something like that happens in my life, I know it is not coincidence, but rather God saying, "Listen up!"

In *Risk the Real,* a stunning little book by Allen Arnold, the author reminds us that fruit always reveals its root. Arnold's premise is based on Eden's two primary trees around which the rest of the garden grew (Genesis 2:8–9). Tree number one was the Tree of Life and tree number two was the Tree of the Knowledge of Good and Evil. Adam and Eve could eat from any tree in that garden except tree number two. They did, and that tree's fruit has been reproducing ever since—death. Death of dreams, relationships, hopes, and eventually the physical body.

The root-fruit connection comes to life in Laura Frantz's historical romance novel *Courting Morrow Little.* Frontier life was dangerous in the 1700s and settlers lost loved ones in cultural conflicts. The heroine's preacher father chooses forgiveness rather than resentment. Her close friend refuses to forgive, and spreads bitterness to everyone around her.

The third book I'm reading is the Bible. In Deuteronomy, God lays out two choices for his people: obedience and disobedience. Life and blessings or life without God.

I am making this covenant with you so that
no one among you — no man,
woman, clan, or tribe — will turn away from the LORD
our God to worship these gods
of other nations, and so that no root among you
bears bitter and poisonous fruit.

Deuteronomy 29:18

It doesn't take much to nurture a small seed of bitterness. It afflicts not only the host but also infects everyone it comes in contact with. Poison is poison, no matter how it's packaged. And things eventually die from exposure to it — friendships, affection, trust.

I'd rather not have pumpkins in my roses, but I really don't want bitterness in my heart.

Lord, help me choose Your way. Help me let go of bitterness and choose life. Amen.

Watch out that no poisonous root of bitterness grows up to trouble you, corrupting many.

Hebrews 12:15

Day Eighty

Our Shelter

Be merciful to me, O God, be merciful to me!
For my soul trusts in You;
and in the shadow of Your wings
I will make my refuge,
until these calamities have passed by.

Psalm 57:1 NKJV

The morning I opened my Bible to Psalm 57 I had just read a social media post from a young woman in a war-torn country.

She recounted miracles and unexplained accounts of things happening that should not have — but for the power of prayer.

She thanked believers around the world who were praying for her countrymen and begged that they would continue. For God could do the impossible, she said, and save the weak and defenseless from the oppressor.

I thought of the innocents who suffer in not only military attacks but in social conflicts and the

brutal assaults of hunger, poverty, and human traf-
ficking. The oppressor dons many different coats,
some as deceptively plain as depression, discouragement, and hopelessness.

Regardless of our battle, the Lord is our shelter
in uncertain times.

"I will cry out to God Most High," Psalm 57:2
(NKJV) says. The words were originally penned by
David, who fled from one who was an associate,
close in family and profession. One who should
have been an ally but was not.

David writes of God sending out His mercy
and truth, and in the next breath, he bemoans his
dangerous situation.

Again, praise follows, with more description
of danger.

Back and forth the psalm goes, from praise
to fear to praise. But it ends in exaltation of God:
"Let Your glory be above all the earth" (Psalm 52:11
NKJV).

This psalm shows me the entwining of cries
for help with cries of confidence, the braiding of
praise and petition.

I see that it is not a faithless heart that express-
es fear to God Almighty. I don't have to couch my
petitions in pretty language but can cry my guts out
before my Creator.

This week, and in the weeks to come, may we lift to God our suffering loved ones as well as others we don't know. The Lord of heaven's armies sends His warriors where mere humans would fall.

Oh, God, thank You that we can be honest with You, crying out in pain for mercy as well as offering our praise. We adore You. Amen.

God is a refuge for us.

Psalm 62:8 NKJV

Day Eighty-One

Forgiveness

Forgive us our sins,
as we forgive those who sin against us.

Luke 11:4

A stomach bug, the flu, or whatever the latest identifier was, stopped by for a visit. During its stay, more than my body was affected. The weakness— or its agent of delivery—made impressions on my groggy mind.

Those days were dark, and too many times my dreams circled back to an offense I thought I'd let go of. Recurring impressions stirred through me of how unjustified the offense was. How wrong and unfair the lie that besmirched someone close to me.

I knew both sides of the story and had wrestled with "letting go," trusting Him whose vengeance is greater than mine to handle the situation. But I hadn't seen that happen yet.

The need for justification became as oppressive as my ailment. The offense/lie was not only perpetrated by a family member, but it was believed by others who should have known better. In my fervor, I formulated a perfect case as though I were a prosecuting attorney.

Through such a perfect argument, was God talking to me, telling me to approach the person who had wounded me the deepest and lay out the facts? Was He directing me to take steps, to go after the offending party and point out their failure to ferret out the truth?

Someone had been unfairly lied about, and it was my duty to defend them. Right? But how was I to know who was filling me with this impulse and giving me such perfect points to make? How could I know if it was God?

The answer came clearly and simply:

Go to His Word. God's personal directive will never contradict His written Word.

Scriptures flooded my groggy brain.

If anyone slaps you on the right cheek,
turn to them the other cheek also.

(Matthew 5:38–40 NIV)

If you do not forgive others their sins,
your Father will not forgive your sins.

(Matthew 6:15 NIV)

Jesus's words carried healing. I could rest on them, or I could press on in what I believed was righteous indignation. The choice was mine.

I desperately wanted to attack. I didn't want to submit to the Lord's clear command. But when I did, a weight lifted and my spirit lightened.

It was very simple. Not easy, but simple.

I do not credit the sickness as either the cause or effect of my spiritual struggle during those dark days. But it plowed the ground for a second sowing of whatever I allowed.

Unforgiveness has the ability to fetter us if we let it. It can tie us up in knots.

I chose freedom. I chose forgiveness. And that's the kicker. Forgiveness is a choice, not a feeling.

Thank You, Lord, for the freedom of forgiveness. Help us give it to others as You give it to us. Amen.

The LORD gives righteousness and justice
to all who are treated unfairly.

Psalm 103:6

Day Eighty-Two

He Leads Me

The LORD alone led him; no foreign god was with him.
Deuteronomy 32:12 NIV

Would you follow someone you didn't know along a path in the woods?

My guess is you wouldn't, because it's all about trust.

Lately, the Twenty-Third Psalm has been pursuing me. It pops up in music on the radio. It's mentioned on social media or in books I'm reading. But most of all, I sense the constant rhythm of its promises in my heart. Like a breeze murmuring through an aspen tree—wooing, soothing. As if God is whispering to me personally. I would follow Him through the woods because I trust Him.

In one of my books, a cowboy character speaks his own version of Psalm 23 at a graveside:

The Lord is my shepherd. I shall not want.

He beds me down in pastures with sweet water.
He leads me on a good trail
and stays with me in the tight places.
And the Lord's spread will be my home forever.[1]

My characterization of that cowboy made me want to write my own personal version:

My Shepherd leads me in the right way.
He takes me to His living water and bread of life.
When it's so dark I can't see Him, He is there.
I feel the brush of His arm against me,
His breath on my hair when He leans close.
Even when I sit with those who hate me,
He feeds me His favor.
He gives me more than enough.
Mercy trails me like a faithful dog.
When I glance over my shoulder,
it looks me in the eye.
The Shepherd promises that I am His,
and I will be His forever.

Take a few minutes and write out your version of Psalm 23 on the lines below. Tape a copy to your

---

[1] Davalynn Spencer, *An Improper Proposal* (Colorado: Wilson Creek Publishing, 2017).

bathroom mirror or put it in your wallet. Make it your own.

Thank You, Lord, that Your Word can be mine. Thank You that I can trust You. Amen.

_____

_____

_____

_____

_____

Day Eighty-Three

Willing to Be Willing

*A man with leprosy came and knelt before him and said,
"Lord, if you are willing, you can make me clean."*

Matthew 8:22 NIV

How do you feel after a long day of interacting with people, most of whom want something from you? It can be exhausting.

Personally, I want to get away, spend quiet time alone. Recharge, pray, get my balance. But that doesn't always happen.

One recent morning, I read Matthew 14 and was struck by how approachable and positive Jesus was. Loosely paraphrased, here's what I saw:

> **Setting**: Small inland sea at night; high wind; boatful of weary men sent ahead of their leader to the other side of the lake. They start seeing things.

> **Jesus**: (Walking on water toward the boat) "Hey guys, I'm here!"
>
> **Peter**: (In the boat) "If it's really you, tell me I can come out there too."
>
> **Jesus**: "Sure, come on!"
>
> **Peter**: (Jumps out, walks across the waves) "Cool!" (Suddenly *notices* the waves.) "Help!"
>
> **Jesus**: (Saves Peter) "Why didn't you trust me?"

Everyone belittles the wet fisherman because he doubted, yet he was the only man willing to get out of the boat. Things could have gone a lot differently.

> **Jesus**: "I'm here. What's taking you so long?"
>
> **Peter**: "If it's really you, tell me I can come out there too."
>
> **Jesus**: "No, you can't do it. You'll sink. Maybe another time."
>
> **Peter**: "But you're always saying—"
>
> **Jesus**: "Hurry up. I've got places to go, people to heal."

Thankfully, Jesus wasn't too busy to take a minute. Do you think He knew Peter was going to sink? I'm sure He did. But He also knew Peter was willing.

Jesus, too, was willing. He didn't discourage Peter because He knew what was possible. I think He wanted Peter and the others to know it too.

Peter walked on the water a lot longer than his companions in the boat. He walked on the water a lot longer than I have. Like his friends, I've never even tried.

Jesus is willing, but are we? He knows what we can do when we trust Him. He knows what is possible. What is He asking us to do that we think we can't?

- Get out of the car and lend a hand?
- Tell someone else about Him?
- Forgive a certain individual?
- Tithe?

Lord, please make me willing to be willing. Amen.

Then Peter called to him, "Lord, if it's really you, tell me to come to you, walking on the water."

Matthew 14:28

Day Eighty-Four

Give and Take

Give, and it will be given to you.
A good measure, pressed down, shaken together
and running over, will be poured into your lap.
For with the measure you use,
it will be measured to you.

Luke 6:38 NIV

Life is full of give and take—sharing. It's a back-and-forth effort like a swing at the playground.

But as is often the case in the English language, there can be a play on the words *give* and *take*.

Are we *giving* people a piece of our mind and *taking* offense?

Are we finding the least of all discoveries—fault?

Remember the old adage, "Finders keepers, losers weepers"? That catchy phrase has a rhyming rhythm that makes it hard to forget. Advertisers charge big bucks for such pithy phrases because they stick in consumers' minds and usually lead to a purchase.

Some words are like that—they stick. Have you noticed? Sometimes they stick like lint.

Or a kiss.

Or Velcro.

Or a dart.

Pointed words often have a barb on the end that keeps us from brushing them off. Maybe that's why it's so easy to take offense when we're in a conversation that makes us feel like a dart board.

I'm intrigued by phrases like *take offense* and *find fault*. Our language constructs them in the active voice, making them something that a person does.

Is it possible to abstain from those two activities?

I believe it is. But *not* doing something is like going on a diet or giving up a bad habit. It creates a vacuum that wants to suck in everything in sight. This is why it is often easier to *not do* one thing if we can *do* something else in its place.

God gave us a great escape from the vacuum of not taking offense. The New Testament teacher Paul told believers to make their conversation always full of grace (Colossians 4:6 NIV). *The Message* version reads, "Be gracious in your speech."

So we have a choice about how to respond in our give-and-take world.

We can *give* graciousness—grace.
We can *take* a minute to consider the heart behind a hurtful word.

And like the back-and-forth playground swing, we can *give* others the chance to find forgiveness in our *take* on things.

Lord, the temptation to answer in kind to an unkind word is so strong. Please help me turn the tide of hurtfulness with a gentle word. Amen.

Never pay back evil with more evil.
Do things in such a way
that everyone can see you are honorable.

Romans 12:17

Day Eighty-Five

Speak, Lord

My soul waits for the LORD
more than those who watch for the morning.

Psalm 130:6 NKJV

I couldn't sleep. It was just after four.

A regular occurrence lately, this time I got up and stepped outside. Above me, Orion stood in full armor, arrow and sword at the ready. And something else. I sensed it in the starry dark before I saw the movement. A deer.

Also bearing full armor, the antlered buck strode silently across the yard, mere feet from me, as if to say, "I'm here. You're safe."

Later, I told a friend what happened and she said, "He's your sentinel."

In those days of living alone, I accepted all such instances as God's way of assuring me He was with me.

When you find yourself wide awake in the early predawn, what do you do?

If you leave for work at that time of day/night, then I already know what you do and my heart goes out to you. But if you typically rise at a more humane hour, what do you do if you pop awake at two or three or four a.m.? Do you rehash the day behind you, or mentally rearrange the furniture in your living room? Do you get up and eat a bowl of oatmeal or half a package of cookies? Or do you scroll through social media on your phone?

Sleeplessness is an ancient and unwelcome nighttime visitor, but I've learned I handle it better when I seek the Lord instead of distraction.

In the Old Testament we read the story of a young boy who awakens because his master, an old priest, calls him. Three times the boy goes to the priest and says, "Here I am. What do you want?" Three times the priest says, "I didn't call you. Go back to bed."

But the third time he realizes that God is speaking to the boy. The priest tells him, "If it happens again, say, 'Speak, Lord, your servant is listening.'"

It did, and the account can be found in 1 Samuel 3:1–18.

I believe that God sometimes wakes us in the night or early morning because that's when we can hear Him. The world isn't accosting us with its distractions and noise. But how many times do we toss and turn or fret about circumstances in our life rather than listen for His voice? What might happen if we listened—not to the worries and fear, but to Him?

What if we said, "Speak, Lord, Your servant is listening."

Our children or grandchildren probably don't talk to us if they think we're not paying attention. Neither do our spouses if they know we're too preoccupied to really listen. Why would God speak to us—at any time of day or night--if He knows we're not listening?

He could have comfort or direction for us. He might want us to pray for someone. What if we waited for Him to whisper a name or give us an impression?

The Father has said, "Be still, and know that I am God" (Psalm 46:10 NIV). Let's try it.

Lord, thank You for caring enough to speak to me. Help me quiet myself and listen. Amen.

Be swift to hear.
James 1:19 NKJV

Day Eighty-Six

Holding Up or Holding On

So do not fear, for I am with you; do not be dismayed,
for I am your God. I will strengthen you and help you;
I will uphold you with my righteous right hand.

Isaiah 41:10 NIV

Have you ever been asked, "How are you holding up?"

Rarely do people mean, "How are you holding up the bank?" or "How are you holding up your socks?"

The idiomatic expression of "How are you holding up?" is used to check on someone's well-being after a trying situation, disease, or tragedy.

The last time someone asked how I was holding up was several years ago following my husband's traumatic brain injury. He fell and never came home. My answer to the question of "holding up" came without consideration: "By holding on."

I didn't see that reply coming and I hadn't given the answer any previous thought. It simply bobbed out of my mouth because it was anchored to my heart.

The phrase *holding up* insinuates personal stamina, vigor, and jaw-clenching determination. At the time, I had none of that.

Holding on says something entirely different. It points to strength and solidity outside oneself.

All I could do was hold on during the eight years my husband lived—no, existed—in full-time nursing care, paralyzed and mentally disabled. During those years, I continued to write about the Lord's unfailing love, and those writings fill the pages of this collection.

I discovered my purpose and calling during those days—to proclaim God and His faithfulness.

I discovered my most valuable possession—the peace of His presence that cannot be counterfeited or confiscated.

And I discovered what was most important to me—hearing Him. For then I would know how to pray for my children and family, and I would know what words to use in my books.

I didn't have the strength to hold up under life's pressures and disappointments. I still don't. But I can hold on for dear life by holding onto the One who holds onto me. His grip is much stronger than mine, and He never lets go.

We all hold onto something or someone. What matters most is who or what it is.

Thank You, Lord, for never letting go of me. You always hold me. Amen.

> *Yet I am always with you;*
> *you hold me by my right hand.*

Psalm 73:23 NIV

Day Eighty-Seven

Grief: The Intimacy of Suffering
Part 1 of 3

. . . through the darkest valley . . .

Psalm 23:4

Everyone faces grief at some point. There is no right, better, or perfect way to deal with it; we just deal with it. But there are little broken bits, fragments that we share in common. You may find my fragments familiar, unusual, or unbelievable. But I pray you find them comforting.

~

I wanted it to be over.
Let me rephrase that:
I *REALLY* wanted it to be *OVER*.
I was tired of hurting and just plain tired.
But—don't you love the buts in life?—the painful, lonely days were days I had to go through. Part of the process.

I remember falling to my knees in my living room one evening, my heart bleeding out through my eyes and dripping into my hands.

And in that surreal moment of knowing Jesus was near, I felt His breath on my hair.

"Really?" someone later asked. "Did you really feel His breath on your hair?"

Yes.

Which is more real—the physical, limited realm in which I exist or the realm of His soul-peace in which I live?

During those earliest days of suffering, I experienced His nearness in ways I had not known before I was alone.

It is the aloneness I kicked against, that valley I didn't want to walk through—

No, wait. I didn't walk. I crawled.

There was no shortcut. I had to go through the valley of shadow alone.

I know, I know—I wasn't really alone, you say. But in the valley, I *felt* alone . . . except for the staff of the Shepherd I kept bumping up against in the dark, that *breath on my hair*.

Everything was so different and I didn't like it. But still the Shepherd set a place for me at the table.

He fed me when I didn't want to eat. Especially not with my enemies lurking nearby—

       fear   longing   depression

Yet, the valley was where I discovered the intimacy of suffering—that precious gift found only there.

So I waited.

Grief isn't something you get over; it's something you get through.

Like a valley.

Oh, God, I need Your help. Amen.

I wait for the LORD, My soul waits.
And in His word do I hope.

Psalm 130:5 NKJV

Day Eighty-Eight

Grief: Sorrow Shared
Part 2 of 3

Weep with those who weep.

Romans 12:15

During the years of my husband's paralysis and traumatic-brain-injury issues, it became more and more difficult for me to attend funerals, so I stopped. I stopped because if I fell apart in public, I wouldn't be able to carry all of me to the car without dropping something.

It wasn't the grief of the families that bothered me. It was the freedom of their loved one who had passed into the presence of Jesus. It was that person's liberation. The severing of painful and unbearable earthly shackles that I . . . resented.

It took me a long time to realize what it was.

My husband was still imprisoned. I grieved because the man I'd known was gone yet he wasn't. I grieved when I visited his care facility and he didn't know me. I grieved anew when COVID quarantines took the visits away.

Isolation dominated my grief, because there were only certain people I wanted to share it with and General Public was not one of them.

Fellow members of a small-group Bible study had come to the out-of-town hospital the night of my husband's accident. They brought what I needed—themselves. Their listening ears.

Those who were close to me carried my pain. They didn't preach platitudes or give me advice—though a retired nurse and mother of many told me to rest because I was going to need it. She was right.

As days stretched into months and years, a friend regularly called from out of state, let me cry the ugly cry, and then prayed for me over the phone. Another sent a note that said, "Lifting you up." She had no idea what that meant to me.

The most comforting words were "I understand." I rarely needed more. It somehow helped redistribute the burden without requiring me to respond graciously.

At church, I wanted to melt into the flooring unnoticed. Disappear into a pew and not talk. Not share. Not have to smile and nod. I wanted the music to lift me on the voices of other worshippers as I offered my personal sacrifice: a broken heart.

But not everyone is like me. Grief is too personal for generalities.

For some, it is easier to share with strangers, and they find help in grief counseling or groups at hospice, nursing homes, and churches.

I discovered the double edge of Galatians 6:2 about bearing the burdens of others. It cut both ways. Even as we grieve, we can look outside ourselves and find people in need and in pain.

We don't have to bombard them (please don't). We can pour into their lives anonymously, if necessary. We can pray for them. Find out what needs to be done and do it. Send a note. Listen.

That is sorrow shared.

Lord, teach us how to weep with those who weep. Amen.

Bear one another's burdens,
and so fulfill the law of Christ.

Galatians 6:2 NKJV

Day Eighty-Nine

Grief: The Healing Place
Part 3 of 3

Blessed are those who mourn,
for they will be comforted.

Matthew 5:4 NIV

I loved the fact that *mourning* and *morning* sounded alike. One expressed sorrow and the other represented a new beginning. Together, they pretty much summed up my condition as I faced the future.

Countless times, I'd been asked, "How are you doing?"

What does one say to that?

> Fine.
> Okay.
> So-so.
> All right.
> Wretched.
> Wonderful.
> Dying on the inside.

Why do you want to know?

Do you truly want to know?

The real answer came to me one . . . *morning*: "I'm in His hands."

My reply set some people on their heels. A few agreed, and several looked puzzled. But everyone heard me.

There was nothing better to say and there was no other place I wanted to be.

When I'm in His hands, I don't have to be fine. I don't have to understand. I don't have to have answers. I can, like a child, lean back against Him and let go. "Your will be done, not mine."

Your will. Two very powerful words. They ring with surrender.

The first night I was alone, I curled up on the floor in front of the woodstove. Six inches of snow skirted my house and temperatures huddled beneath a twenty-degree blanket.

The woodstove was a safe and quiet place.

Fire danced behind the glass door and, in time, became a companion of sorts—something warm and alive that I could sit near and watch each evening. Something from which I drew comfort.

I slept and ate and prayed and wrote before that fire.

I also sang and played my guitar.

One evening I sensed the Lord there listening, *at my right hand,* and I moved my chair over to make room for Him.

Sound silly?

I didn't see Him, didn't hear Him, but I knew He was there.

How many times in my life had I moved something out of the way to make room for Jesus?

How many times had I not?

That night in front of the woodstove with the fire glowing through the glass, I sang to Him. Old songs, new songs, most of them quiet and gentle because that was how I felt. It seemed I'd spent only a little while in His presence, yet when I looked at the clock, two hours had passed.

Would eternity be like that?

The rug in front of the woodstove became a healing place, and I felt God approved.

Long before I existed, He had told Moses, "Here is a place by Me" (Exodus 33:21 NKJV). He went on to say that He would cover Moses with His hand. So Moses waited in that place.

No substitute can be found for waiting on the Lord, but it requires trust.

Trust is often just doing the next thing—like the dishes. The laundry. Mowing the yard or stacking firewood. The next thing can be salvation when

I take a step forward, trusting that He will sweep up the pieces if I fall.

Grief breaks into our lives whether we are ready or not. Usually, we are not. And there are triggers after the fact. Will there ever not be?

Pain sneaks up on us when we're not looking. But God is the Great Recycler of Human Wreckage. He knows how to fit the pieces back together and make them stronger.

When I finally went to a funeral after swearing them off, it was my husband's Celebration of Life, eight years after he fell. I was amazed at how I felt when people showed up. They honored him with their presence and thereby comforted me. I didn't know that would happen, and it showed me how important it was to share another's loss.

My husband, Mike, died during the peak of rodeo season—fitting, in my opinion. For he had spent twenty-five years as a rodeo clown and bull-fighter, working countless rodeos across the country. He loved the work, the people, the sport of rodeo.

Just before his service, my pastor told me that mourning was one of the ways we showed our love. I liked that. It gave me permission to let go of my pent-up grief.

Jesus said those who mourn would be comforted. That didn't mean I wouldn't miss or continue to love Mike; it meant comfort awaited.

Life goes on, they say, and it does. It just goes on differently.

Jesus goes with us.

He is with us each day—if we allow Him to get that close—walking with us through the triggers and the pain, whispering His peace as we lie down at night.

And He is there in the morning, waiting for us.

Just like He was in the valley.

Oh, God, thank You. You have seen me through it all. Amen.

Weeping may last through the night,
but joy comes with the morning.

Psalm 30:5

Day Ninety

Hope and a Future

Eye has not seen, nor ear heard,
nor have entered into the heart of man
the things which God has prepared
for those who love Him.

1 Corinthians 2:9 NKJV

Faced with the first, unmarked page of a new journal, I smooth the paper, savoring its fresh, unmarred surface. Journals segment my life. They line a shelf in my office, filled with personal accounts of success and failure, victories and mishaps, prayers and Bible verses.

Journaling helps me see what I'm thinking. It's my process. I self-medicate with words, but I know it's not for everyone. It's not a one-size-fits-all solution.

That's one of the things I love about God—He is personal. The God of one as well as the God of millions.

For me, a new journal represents the juncture of known and unknown. I want to make smart choices, especially when it comes to facing hard times, and hard times are sure to come.

When I'm in the midst of pain, it's hard to see what lies ahead. Fear wants to slither in and choke me down, but Jesus steps in with his well-traveled feet and crushes the serpent.

I saw a representation of those feet up close years ago during our church's rendition of the Passion Play. I had the role of the sinful woman who washed Jesus's feet and dried them with her hair (Luke 7:37–47). You can't get much closer than that.

At the crucifixion scene, I stood at the base of the cross and again saw those feet, theatrically made up to appear wounded and bleeding. The image will forever remain in my memory—Jesus dying for *me*. You can't get more personal than that.

More recently, I was in another play with the part of the sick and bleeding woman who secretly touched Jesus's hem believing that she would be healed (Mark 5:25–34). But Jesus didn't let it remain secret. He wanted to see her, make certain that everyone else saw her and recognized her faith put into action. Again, He demonstrated His love of the one and not just the many.

He is that personal.

Ask God to show you His purpose for your life. Ask Him to show you how to align your life with His plan. Spend time in His Word, for it has the keys to life, regardless of your situation or where you are. He is the God of one and He loves you more than you know.

God doesn't promise us tomorrow, only eternity if we choose Him.

Prayerfully consider, listening for His whisper and watching for His direction. When you find it, and you will, write it here for encouragement:

My purpose

_____

_____

_____

_____

Most valued possession

_____

_____

_____

_____

Most important to me

_____

_____

_____

_____

"For I know the plans I have for you,"
declares the Lord,
"plans to prosper you and not to harm you,
plans to give you hope and a future."

Jeremiah 29:11 NIV

Because He is at my right hand, I am not alone.

Acknowledgments

Thank you for reading *At My Right Hand.* I pray you are encouraged in your own walk by these story-devotions.

Great love and gratitude go to my husband, Pastor George Casias; my children and their families; editor Christy Distler; Jill Maple; Suzie Veatch; and to the King of my heart and God of my gifts, Jesus Messiah.

Our God is faithful and true. I urge you to search the treasures of His Word and make His ways your ways. The more you get to know Him, the more you will see His footprints in the world around you.

Author's Note

I wrote little about my personal struggle with grief until the year following the home-going of my late husband, Mike. I couldn't write about it during those long years of what I called widowhood, only after. Only as I saw my friend, Pastor George Casias, go through emotions similar to mine following the long illness and loss of his wife. I shared with him about the valley, and he shared about the sense of leaving a loved one "behind" as we move on with our lives.

I understood what he meant. I had felt it myself. But God comforted me one morning about that, and I felt led to share it with George. We can't leave a deceased loved one behind because they have gone on ahead of us. When David's infant son died, David rose from his grieving, removed his garments of mourning, and went about his calling in life. The child would not come back to David, but David would go to him (2 Samuel 12:23). Always he would love the child, but God drew him away from the dark corner of grief and into the light of living.

This is what the Lord has done for George and me, and we rejoice in His compassion and provision. Who else but God could give us a new marriage, a new partnership in the Lord at this point in our lives?

"Your will, Lord," we prayed, hands off and ready to go on alone if that was His will. But it wasn't. He poured love into our hearts and blessed us by giving us fresh life and new opportunities to trust. God's timing is perfect, and His plan so much better than ours.

About the Author

Davalynn Spencer's story-devotions have appeared in multiple publications, including *Chicken Soup for the Soul* and Guideposts' *All God's Creatures* and *Miracles Do Happen.* She is an internationally renowned, multi-published author of inspirational Western romance, an award-winning former journalist, and a sought-after writing instructor. She and George make their home along the Front Range of Colorado's Rocky Mountains. Contact her via her website at www.davalynnspencer.com

Find more inspiration with Davalynn's first collection of 90 story-devotions, *Always Before Me.*

~May all that you read be uplifting.~

www.ingramcontent.com/pod-product-compliance
Lightning Source LLC
Chambersburg PA
CBHW021710120626
46545CB00004B/1484